초등
영어 읽기

2

초등 영어 읽기 2

초판발행 2020년 12월 21일

글쓴이 Contents Tree
그린이 정혜선, 조서아, 윤희재
엮은이 송지은, 진혜정, 김한나
기획 한동오
펴낸이 엄태상
영문감수 Kirsten March
디자인 진지화
오디오 전진우
마케팅 본부 이승욱, 전한나, 왕성석, 노원준, 조인선, 조성민
경영기획 마정인, 최성훈, 정다운, 김다미, 오희연
제작 전태준
물류 정종진, 윤덕현, 양희은, 신승진
펴낸곳 시소스터디
주소 서울시 종로구 자하문로 300 시사빌딩
주문 및 문의 1588-1582
팩스 02-3671-0510
홈페이지 www.sisabooks.com/siso
이메일 sisostudy@sisadream.com
등록번호 제2019-000149호
ISBN 979-11-970830-9-9 63740

진 짜 진 짜

초등 영어 읽기

②

Introduction

★ 〈진짜 진짜 초등 영어 읽기〉 이렇게 학습해 보세요.

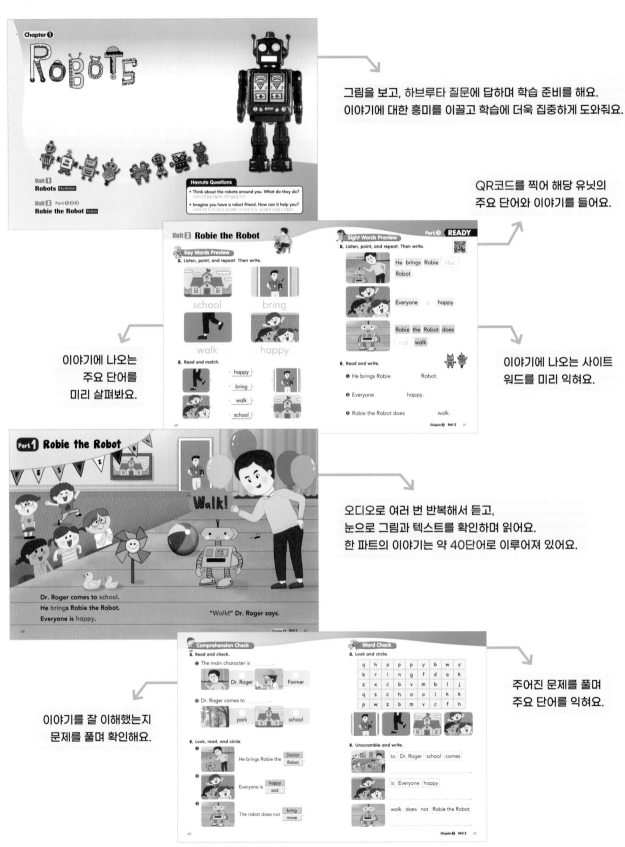

그림을 보고, 하브루타 질문에 답하며 학습 준비를 해요.
이야기에 대한 흥미를 이끌고 학습에 더욱 집중하게 도와줘요.

QR코드를 찍어 해당 유닛의
주요 단어와 이야기를 들어요.

이야기에 나오는
주요 단어를
미리 살펴봐요.

이야기에 나오는 사이트
워드를 미리 익혀요.

오디오로 여러 번 반복해서 듣고,
눈으로 그림과 텍스트를 확인하며 읽어요.
한 파트의 이야기는 약 40단어로 이루어져 있어요.

주어진 문제를 풀며
주요 단어를 익혀요.

이야기를 잘 이해했는지
문제를 풀며 확인해요.

 하브루타 가이드의 안내에 따라 워크북을 학습하며 **영어 실력** 뿐 아니라 **생각하는 힘**도 키워요!

알고 있는 단어와 모르는 단어를 체크 해요. 아는 것과 모르는 것을 정확히 파악하는 것만으로도 학습 효과는 눈에 띄게 달라요. (메타인지 효과)

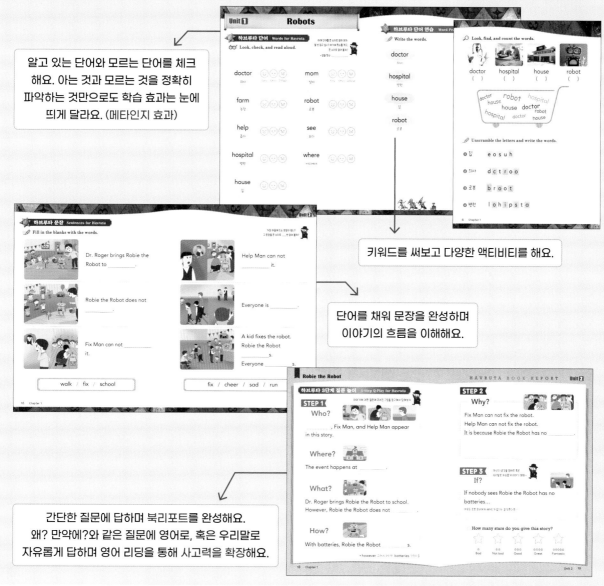

키워드를 써보고 다양한 액티비티를 해요.

단어를 채워 문장을 완성하며 이야기의 흐름을 이해해요.

간단한 질문에 답하며 북리포트를 완성해요. 왜? 만약에?와 같은 질문에 영어로, 혹은 우리말로 자유롭게 답하며 영어 리딩을 통해 사고력을 확장해요.

 학습 안내 동영상을 확인하세요.

하브루타가 뭐예요?

하브루타란 서로 짝을 지어 질문하고 대답하면서 생각을 나누는 유대인의 전통 토론법이에요. 그 어느 누구와도 짝을 이룰 수 있겠지만, 학습 영역에서 그 짝은 함께 공부하는 친구들, 혹은 교사와 학생, 부모와 자녀로 이루어집니다.

 ## 하브루타 워크북 사용 설명서

1. 나의 하브루타 스터디 플랜: 오늘 학습할 내용을 확인해요.

2. 하브루타 단어: 단어를 큰 소리로 읽어 보며 쉬운 단어, 어려운 단어들을 체크해요.

3. 하브루타 단어 연습: 키워드를 손으로 여러 번 써보고, 연습 문제를 풀며 단어를 외워요.

4. **하브루타 3단계 질문 놀이:**

   Step 1. Who?(누가?), Where?(어디서?), What?(무엇을?), How?(어떻게?)에 답해요.

   Step 2. 읽은 내용을 바탕으로 Why?(왜?)에 답해봅니다.

   Step 3. 새로운 가정에 대해 자유롭게 상상하면서 If?(만약에?)에 답해요.

하브루타 가이드

각 코너마다 등장하는 하브루타 가이드의 질문에 답하며 학습을 진행하세요. 자연스럽게 하브루타식 워크북 활동을 할 수 있어요. 질문과 답이 꼭 영어일 필요는 없어요. 영어는 실력에 맞게 활용하되, 확장된 질문과 답을 자유롭게 하면 비판적으로 사고하는 능력을 키울 수 있어요.

★ ★ 추천서 ★ ★

◇◇◇

『진짜 진짜 초등 영어 읽기』는 우리나라가 도입해야 할 하브루타식 질문이 자연스럽게 녹아 있는 탁월한 영어 리딩 학습서입니다. 하브루타라는 이름으로 창의적인 사고훈련과 공부법, 가족 대화법을 교육하는 전문가의 한사람으로서 우리 아이들에게 꼭 필요한 영어 학습서인『진짜 진짜 초등 영어 읽기』를 추천합니다.

생각할 거리가 풍성하게 담겨있는 재미있는 이야기들은 단순한 패턴 반복식 영어 리딩의 한계를 극복하고 하브루타식 학습법으로 공부하기에 적합합니다. 이야기가 시작되기 전부터 흥미와 관심을 끄는 질문으로 아이들이 이야기에 집중하게 만들고, 단순히 학습의 흐름을 따라가는 것이 아니라 주도적으로 생각하며 이야기를 읽게 만듭니다. 또, 글을 읽은 후에는 사실 확인을 위한 질문 뿐 아니라 더 깊게 생각해 봐야할 질문을 통해 생각을 자극합니다. 아이들은 하브루타 학습법으로 공부하면서 영어 실력 뿐 아니라 생각하는 힘을 기를 수 있습니다.

워크북의 코너 곳곳에 마련된 질문들은 메타인지 효과로 학습자로 하여금 자신의 공부 모습을 들여다보게 합니다. 내가 알고 있는 것과 모르는 것을 정확히 아는 것만으로도 학습의 효과는 눈에 띄게 다릅니다. 생각을 자극하고 학습에 집중하게 하는 질문들을 읽고 답하는 것만으로도 하브루타 학습의 효과를 누릴 수 있습니다. 하브루타식 학습법이 접목된『진짜 진짜 초등 영어 읽기』에서 창의적으로 생각하고 영어 리딩 실력을 높이시길 바랍니다.

교육학박사
하브루타창의인성교육연구소 소장   장성애

Contents

★ 한 챕터는 같은 소재로 쓰여진 Nonfiction과 Fiction 두 가지 글로 구성되어 있어요. ★

Chapter ❸ Crocodiles

9

ROBOTS

Havruta Questions

- **Think about the robots around you. What do they do?**
  주변에 로봇들을 떠올려봐. 어떤 일들을 하지?

- **Imagine you have a robot friend. How can it help you?**
  너에게 로봇 친구가 있다고 상상해봐. 너의 로봇 친구는 널 어떻게 도와줄 수 있을까?

Unit **1** **Robots**

Key Words Preview

A. Listen, point, and repeat. Then write.

robot

hospital

doctor

house

B. Read and match.

- doctor -
- house -
- hospital -
- robot -

Sight Words Preview

A. Listen, point, and repeat. Then write.

Where do you see robots ?

We see robots in the hospital.

They help farmers.

B. Read and write.

❶ Where _____ you see robots?

❷ We see robots _____ the hospital.

❸ _____ help farmers.

Robots

Where do you see robots?

We see robots in the hospital.

They help doctors.

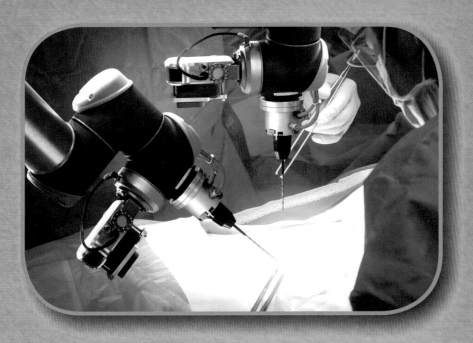

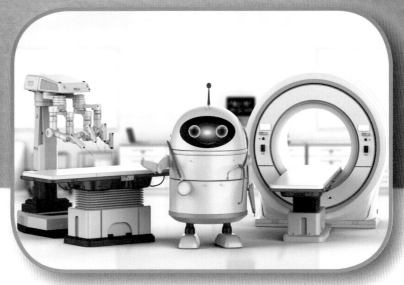

We see robots on the farm.

They help farmers.

We see robots in the house.
They help mom!

Comprehension Check

A. Read and check.

1 This is a story about _____.

 robots    farmers

2 We see robots in the _____.

 hospital    woods

B. Look and check T(True) or F(False).

1
We see robots on the farm.

T ☐   F ☐

2
We see robots in the house.

T ☐   F ☐

3
They help farmers.

T ☐   F ☐

18

Word Check

A. Complete the puzzle.

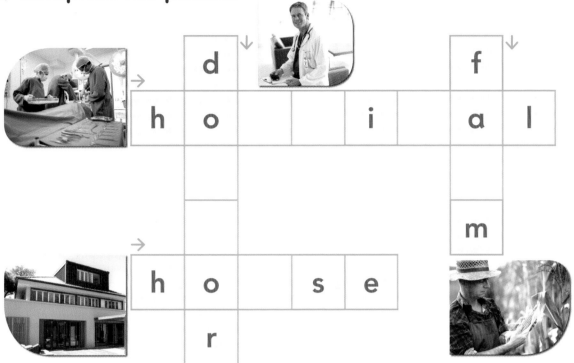

	d					f		
h	o			i		a	l	
						m		
h	o		s	e				
	r							

B. Look, read, and match.

❶ Where do you see

❷ We see robots

❸ They help

in the house.

doctors.

robots?

Unit 2 Robie the Robot

Key Words Preview

A. Listen, point, and repeat. Then write.

school

bring

walk

happy

B. Read and match.

- happy ·
- bring ·
- walk ·
- school ·

Sight Words Preview

A. Listen, point, and repeat. Then write.

He brings Robie ⟦the⟧ Robot.

Everyone ⟦is⟧ happy.

Robie the Robot does ⟦not⟧ walk.

B. Read and write.

❶ He brings Robie _____ Robot.

❷ Everyone _____ happy.

❸ Robie the Robot does _____ walk.

Part 1 Robie the Robot

Dr. Roger comes to school.

He brings Robie the Robot.

Everyone is happy.

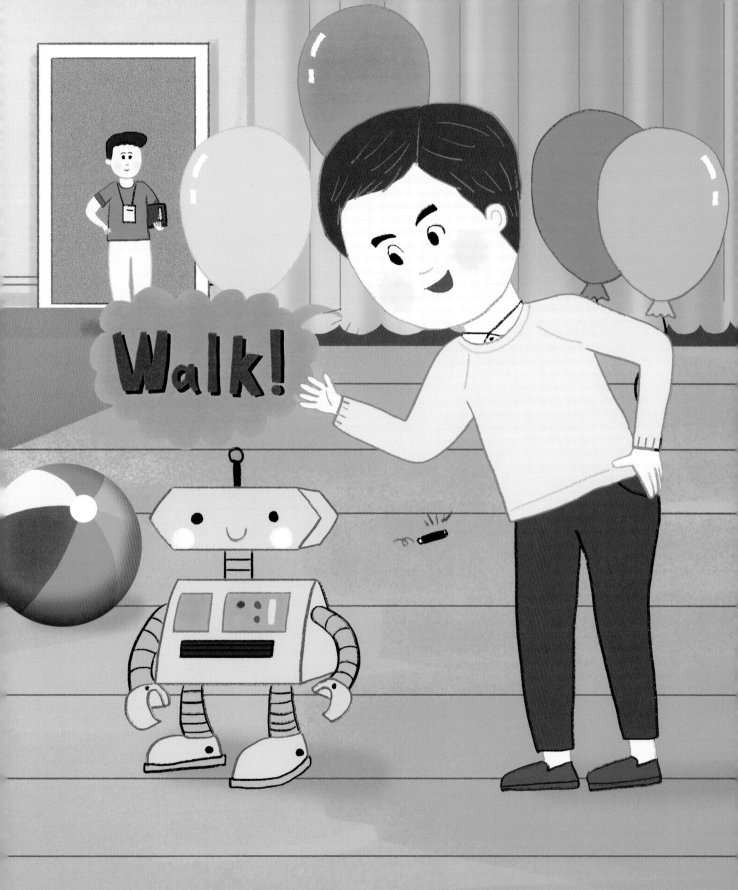

"Walk!" Dr. Roger says.

Robie the Robot does not walk.

"Walk!" Dr. Roger says again.
But the robot does not move.

Comprehension Check

A. Read and check.

1 The main character is _____.

 Dr. Roger  Farmer

2 Dr. Roger comes to _____.

 park  school

B. Look, read, and circle.

1  He brings Robie the 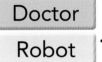 Doctor / Robot .

2  Everyone is 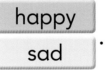 happy / sad .

3  The robot does not bring / move .

26

Word Check

A. Look and circle.

q	h	a	p	p	y	b	w	y
b	r	i	n	g	f	d	a	k
z	x	c	b	v	m	b	l	j
q	s	c	h	o	o	l	k	k
p	w	z	b	m	v	c	f	h

B. Unscramble and write.

| to | Dr. Roger | school | comes |

_____.

| is | Everyone | happy |

_____.

| walk | does | not | Robie the Robot |

_____.

Robie the Robot

Key Words Preview

A. Listen, point, and repeat. Then write.

hurry

call

come

fix

B. Read and match.

- hurry -

- come -

- call -

- fix -

28

Sight Words Preview

A. Listen, point, and repeat. Then write.

Fix Man comes to

school .

But he can not fix it.

But he can not fix it.

B. Read and write.

❶ Fix Man comes _____ school.

❷ _____ he can not fix it.

❸ But _____ can not fix it.

Robie the Robot

"Please hurry!"

Dr. Roger calls Fix Man.

Fix Man comes to school.
But he can not fix it.

"Please hurry!"
Fix Man calls Help Man.

Help Man comes to school.

But he can not fix it.

Comprehension Check

A. Read and check.

❶ Dr. Roger calls _____.

 Fix Man ☐    Robie ☐

❷ _____ comes to school.

 Grandma ☐    Help Man ☐

B. Look, read, and circle.

❶  Fix Man comes to | hospital | school |.

❷  But he can not | fix | call | it.

❸  Fix Man calls | Help Man | Dr. Roger |.

34

A. Look and circle.

 ▶ h u r r y w z q p k

 ▶ t x c v c a l l v x

 ▶ f v c p m q c o m e

 ▶ w q z f i x b v z p

B. Look, read, and match.

1 Fix Man calls   **2** Fix Man comes   **3** Help Man can not

Help Man!

to school.   Help Man.   fix it.

Unit 2 Robie the Robot

Key Words Preview

A. Listen, point, and repeat. Then write.

sad

point

cheer

run

B. Read and match.

point

run

cheer

sad

Sight Words Preview

A. Listen, point, and repeat. Then write.

Everyone is sad.

You fixed it.

Fix Man and Help Man cheer.

B. Read and write.

❶ _____ is sad.

❷ _____ fixed it.

❸ Fix Man _____ Help Man cheer.

Dr. Roger is sad. Everyone is sad.

A kid points and asks,

"What is this?"

"You fixed it!" Dr. Roger cheers.

"You fixed it!"

Fix Man and Help Man cheer.

40

"Run!" Dr. Roger says.
Robie the Robot runs. Everyone cheers.

A. Read and check.

1 "You fixed it!" _____ cheers.

 ☐ Dr. Roger  ☐ Robie

2 Fix Man and Help Man _____.

 ☐ cheer  ☐ call

B. Look, read, and check.

1

☐ A kid points and asks, "What is this?"

☐ A farmer points and asks, "What is this?"

2

☐ Robie the Robot says.

☐ Robie the Robot runs.

3

☐ Everyone cheers.

☐ Everyone is sad.

Word Check

A. Look and circle.

cheer | sad | run

sad | cheer | point

run | point | cheer

point | run | kid

B. Unscramble and write.

fixed | You | it

_____.

sad | Everyone | is

_____.

Robie | runs | Robot | the

_____.

Robie the Robot

Dr. Roger comes to school.

He brings Robie the Robot.

Everyone is happy.

"Walk!" Dr. Roger says.

Robie the Robot does not walk.

"Walk!" Dr. Roger says again.

But the robot does not move.

"Please hurry!"

Dr. Roger calls Fix Man.

Fix Man comes to school.

But he can not fix it.

"Please hurry!"

Fix Man calls Help Man.

Help Man comes to school.

But he can not fix it.

Dr. Roger is sad.

Everyone is sad.

A kid points and asks,

"What is this?"

"You fixed it!" Dr. Roger cheers.

"You fixed it!" Fix Man and

Help Man cheer.

"Run!" Dr. Roger says.

Robie the Robot runs.

Everyone cheers.

Cooking

Havruta Questions

- **Think about what a cook does.**
  요리사가 무슨 일을 하는지 생각해 보자.

- **Imagine you are a cook. What do you want to make?**
  요리사가 되었다고 상상해봐. 뭘 만들고 싶니?

Unit 1 What a Cook Does

Key Words Preview

A. Listen, point, and repeat. Then write.

cook

kitchen

apron

meal

B. Read and match.

- apron
- meal
- kitchen
- cook

Sight Words Preview

A. Listen, point, and repeat. Then write.

Cooks | work | in | the | kitchen .

They | wear | a | hat .

They | make | tasty | meals .

B. Read and write.

1 Cooks work _____ the kitchen.

2 They wear _____ hat.

3 _____ make tasty meals.

What a Cook Does

Cooks work in the kitchen.

They wear a hat.

They wear an apron.

hat

apron

They keep their hands clean.

They keep their **kitchen** clean.

They prepare fresh food.

They make tasty meals.

Comprehension Check

A. Read and check.

❶ This is a story about _____.

 ☐ cooks    ☐ foxes

❷ Cooks work in the _____.

 ☐ farm    ☐ kitchen

B. Look and check T(True) or F(False).

❶  They wear a ring.

T ☐   F ☐

❷  They keep their kitchen clean.

T ☐   F ☐

❸  They make tasty meals.

T ☐   F ☐

Word Check

A. Complete the puzzle.

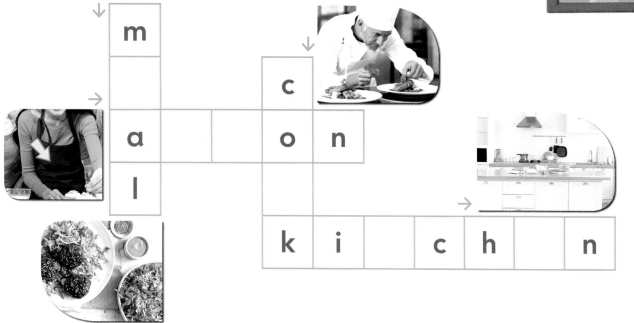

	m				
a			c		
l			o	n	

k | i | | c | h | | n

B. Look, read, and match.

1 Cooks work

2 They wear

3 They prepare

an apron

in the kitchen.

fresh food.

Key Words Preview

A. Listen, point, and repeat. Then write.

ring

finger

sleep

wear

B. Read and match.

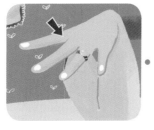

sleep

wear

finger

ring

Sight Words Preview

A. Listen, point, and repeat. Then write.

It twinkles on her finger .

She eats with her ring on .

She plays with her ring on .

B. Read and write.

❶ It twinkles ＿＿＿＿＿ her finger.

❷ She eats ＿＿＿＿＿ her ring on.

❸ She plays with ＿＿＿＿＿ ring on.

Part 1 Pancakes and Mia's Ring

Mia likes her ring.

It twinkles on her finger.

She eats with her ring on.

58

She plays with her ring on.

She sleeps with her ring on.

She wears her ring all the time.

Comprehension Check

A. Read and check.

1 The main character is _____.

Mom ☐   Mia ☐

2 Mia likes her _____.

glasses ☐   ring ☐

B. Look, read, and circle.

1

It twinkles on her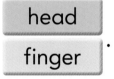
| head |
| finger | .

2

She | plays |
| eats | with her ring on.

3

She | sleeps |
| brings | with her ring on.

Word Check

A. Look and circle.

r	i	n	g	z	x	c	u	w
m	b	p	y	w	v	v	t	e
h	f	i	n	g	e	r	m	a
p	q	w	z	c	b	t	k	r
l	j	g	s	l	e	e	p	k

B. Unscramble and write.

Mia | ring | likes | her

_____.

with | her ring on | She | plays

_____.

She | with | eats | her ring on

_____.

Unit **2** Pancakes and Mia's Ring

Key Words Preview

A. Listen, point, and repeat. Then write.

pour

flour

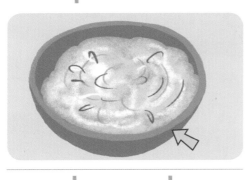

bowl

milk

B. Read and match.

· flour ·

· bowl ·

· milk ·

· pour ·

64

Sight Words Preview

A. Listen, point, and repeat. Then write.

Mia and Mom make pancakes .

Mia pours milk into the bowl .

Now the pancakes are done .

B. Read and write.

❶ Mia _____ Mom make pancakes.

❷ Mia pours milk _____ the bowl.

❸ Now the pancakes _____ done.

Part 2

Pancakes and Mia's Ring

Mia and Mom make pancakes.

Mia pours flour into the bowl.

Mia pours milk into the bowl.

Mia pours sugar into the bowl.

Mia stirs and mixes.

Now the pancakes are done.

Comprehension Check

A. Read and check.

❶ Mia and Mom make _____.

 milk ☐    pancakes ☐

❷ Mia pours sugar into the _____.

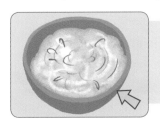 bowl ☐    robot ☐

B. Look, read, and circle.

❶  Mia and Dad / Mom make pancakes.

❷  Mia pours sugar / milk into the bowl.

❸  Mia runs / stirs   and mixes.

Word Check

A. Look and circle.

> h p o **u r** j q g k o

f **l o u r** k z x g t

> z x v c p m **b o w l**

> w **m i l k** u r v z p

B. Look, read, and match.

❶ Mia and Mom make

❷ Mia pours sugar

❸ Now the pancakes are

into the bowl.

done.

pancakes.

Unit 2 Pancakes and Mia's Ring

Key Words Preview

A. Listen, point, and repeat. Then write.

bite

sister

love

cry

B. Read and match.

- bite •
- cry •
- sister •
- love •

Sight Words Preview

A. Listen, point, and repeat. Then write.

Dad bites the pancakes .

We love pancakes !

That is my ring !

B. Read and write.

❶ Dad bites _____ pancakes.

❷ _____ love pancakes!

❸ That is _____ ring!

Part 3 Pancakes and Mia's Ring

Dad bites the pancakes.

Mia's sister, Mina, bites the pancakes.

"We love pancakes!" they say.

"Ouch!" Mina cries.

"That is my ring!" Mia says.

"A cook does not wear a ring," Mom says.

"I'm sorry," Mia says.

Comprehension Check

A. Read and check.

❶ "Ouch!" _____ cries.

 ☐ Dad  ☐ Mina

❷ "That is my _____!" Mia says.

 ☐ ring  ☐ pancakes

B. Look, read, and check.

☐ Dad bites the pancakes.

☐ Mom bites the pancakes.

☐ We love robots!

☐ We love pancakes!

☐ A cook does not wear a ring.

☐ A kid does not wear a ring.

Word Check

A. Look and circle.

| sister | bite | cry |

| cry | love | sister |

| bite | sister | love |

| love | bite | cry |

B. Unscramble and write.

the   Dad   pancakes   bites

_____.

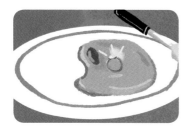

is   That   ring   my

_____!

pancakes   We   love

_____!

Pancakes and Mia's Ring

Mia likes her ring.

It twinkles on her finger.

She eats with her ring on.

She plays with her ring on .

She sleeps with her ring on.

She wears her ring all the time.

Mia and Mom make pancakes.

Mia pours flour into the bowl.

Mia pours milk into the bowl.

Mia pours sugar into the bowl.

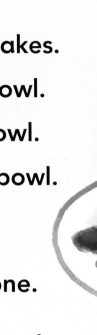

Mia stirs and mixes.

Now the pancakes are done.

Dad bites the pancakes.

Mia's sister, Mina, bites

the pancakes.

"We love pancakes!" they say.

"Ouch!" Mina cries.

"That is my ring!" Mia says.

"A cook does not wear a ring," Mom says.

"I'm sorry," Mia says.

Chapter ③
Crocodiles

Havruta Questions

- **Look at the picture.
  What is the same? What is different?**
  그림을 봐.
  악어와 암탉은 무엇이 같을까? 무엇이 다를까?

Unit **1** Crocodiles

A. Listen, point, and repeat. Then write.

webbed

jaw

hard

fast

B. Read and match.

jaw

webbed

fast

hard

84

Sight Words Preview

A. Listen, point, and repeat. Then write.

Crocodiles [are] big animals.

They [have] a strong jaw.

They live [in] rivers.

B. Read and write.

1 Crocodiles ＿＿＿＿＿＿ big animals.

2 They ＿＿＿＿＿＿ a strong jaw.

3 They live ＿＿＿＿＿＿ rivers.

Crocodiles

Crocodiles are big animals.

They have a strong jaw.

They have four webbed feet.

They have sharp teeth.

They have hard skin.

They live in rivers.

They move very fast.

They hunt very fast.

They can be very dangerous.

Crocodile Safety

DANGER

Crocodiles inhabit this area.
Attacks cause injury or death.

· Do not enter the water.
· Keep away from the water's edge.

Report sightings and incidents to:
Bowali Visitor Centre (08) 8938 1120

kakadu

Comprehension Check

A. Read and check.

❶ This is a story about a _____ .

 ☐ crocodile    ☐ fox

❷ Crocodiles live in _____ .

 ☐ woods    ☐ rivers

B. Look and check T(True) or F(False).

❶  They have a strong jaw.

T ☐   F ☐

❷  They have hard feet.

T ☐   F ☐

❸  They hunt very fast.

T ☐   F ☐

Word Check

A. Complete the puzzle.

```
              h
    j     f a       t

    w e    b    d
```

B. Look, read, and match.

❶ Crocodiles are   ❷ They move   ❸ They have

very fast.   hard skin.   big animals.

Key Words Preview

A. Listen, point, and repeat. Then write.

meet

mouth

open

shut

B. Read and match.

mouth

open

shut

meet

Sight Words Preview

A. Listen, point, and repeat. Then write

Crocodile and Hen meet at the river.

I will eat you !

Crocodile shuts his mouth .

B. Read and write.

❶ Crocodile and Hen meet _____ the river.

❷ I will _____ you!

❸ Crocodile shuts _____ mouth.

Part 1 Crocodile and Hen

One day, Crocodile and Hen
meet at the river.

"I will eat you!" says Crocodile.
Crocodile opens his mouth.

"My brother!" says Hen.

"Don't eat me."

Crocodile shuts his mouth.
"Brother?" Crocodile wonders.

Comprehension Check

A. Read and check.

❶ The main characters are Crocodile and _____.

 ☐ Hen

 ☐ Farmer

❷ "I will eat you!" says _____.

 ☐ Fox

 ☐ Crocodile

B. Look, read, and circle.

❶

Crocodile and Hen meet
at the | river |
| house | .

❷

Crocodile opens his | mouth |
| feet | .

❸

"Brother?" | Crocodile |
| Hen | wonders.

Word Check

A. Look and circle.

x	o	p	e	n	p	w	f	g
z	q	w	a	u	b	z	m	k
p	v	s	h	u	t	d	e	k
p	q	w	i	c	b	t	e	r
m	o	u	t	h	g	m	t	q

B. Unscramble and write.

| his | mouth | opens | Crocodile |

_____.

| eat | Don't | me |

_____.

| mouth | his | Crocodile | shuts |

_____.

Unit 2 Crocodile and Hen

Key Words Preview

A. Listen, point, and repeat. Then write.

water

land

brother

wonder

B. Read and match.

· land ·

· brother ·

· wonder ·

· water ·

Sight Words Preview

A. Listen, point, and repeat. Then write.

I live in water .

You live on land .

You are not my brother .

B. Read and write.

❶ I live _____ water.

❷ You live _____ land.

❸ You _____ not my brother.

Part 2 Crocodile and Hen

"I live in water," says Crocodile.

"You live on land."

"You are not my brother,"
says Crocodile.
"I will eat you!"

"My brother!" says Hen.
"Don't eat me."

"Brother?"
Crocodile wonders.

Comprehension Check

A. Read and check.

1. "I live in _____," says Crocodile.

water ☐   land ☐

2. "My brother!" says _____.

   Hen ☐      Crocodile ☐

B. Look, read, and circle.

1.    You live on 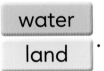 water / land .

2. 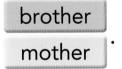   You are not my brother / mother .

3.    Don't move / eat me.

Word Check

A. Look and circle.

h u **w a t e r** q p k

t x **l a n d** b l v x

b r o t h e r z q p

f i x b **w o n d e r**

B. Look, read, and match.

① I live

② You are not

③ I will

my brother.

eat you.

in water.

Unit 2 Crocodile and Hen

Key Words Preview

A. Listen, point, and repeat. Then write.

scale

feather

egg

alike

B. Read and match.

egg

alike

scale

feather

Sight Words Preview

A. Listen, point, and repeat. Then write.

You have feathers .

A hen lays eggs .

We are alike .

B. Read and write.

❶ You _____ feathers.

❷ _____ hen lays eggs.

❸ We _____ alike.

Part 3 Crocodile and Hen

scales

"I have scales," says Crocodile.

"You are not my brother," says Crocodile. "I will eat you!"

feathers

"You have feathers."

"A crocodile lays eggs," says Hen,

"and a hen lays eggs."

"We are alike!"
Hen cries out.
"Goodbye Brother!"

Comprehension Check

A. Read and check.

1 "I have _____," says Crocodile.

 ☐ scales  ☐ feathers

2 "We are alike!" _____ cries out.

 ☐ Crocodile  ☐ Hen

B. Look, read, and check.

1

☐ You have scales.

☐ You have feathers.

2

☐ "You are not my brother," says Crocodile.

☐ "You are not my brother," says Hen.

3

☐ A crocodile lays eggs.

☐ A fox lays eggs.

Word Check

A. Look and circle.

| feather | scale | alike |

| egg | alike | feather |

| scale | feather | egg |

| alike | egg | cry |

B. Unscramble and write.

I   scales   have

_____.

have   feathers   You

_____.

are   We   alike

_____!

Crocodile and Hen

One day, Crocodile and Hen meet at the river.

"I will eat you!" says Crocodile.

Crocodile opens his mouth.

"My brother!" says Hen.

"Don't eat me."

Crocodile shuts his mouth.

"Brother?" Crocodile wonders.

"I live in water," says Crocodile.

"You live on land."

"You are not my brother,"
says Crocodile. "I will eat you!"

"My brother!" says Hen.

"Don't eat me."

"Brother?" Crocodile wonders.

"I have scales," says Crocodile.

"You have feathers."

"You are not my brother,"

says Crocodile. "I will eat you!"

"A crocodile lays eggs," says Hen,

"and a hen lays eggs."

"We are alike!" Hen cries out.

"Goodbye Brother!"

My Word List

alike (아주) 비슷한

"We are _____!" Hen cries out.
(p.113)

apron 앞치마

They wear an _____. (p.51)

bite 베어 물다

Dad _____s the pancakes. (p.74)

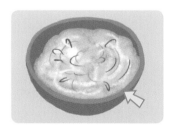

bowl 그릇

Mia pours flour into the _____.
(p.67)

bring 가져오다

He _____s Robie the Robot.
(p.22)

brother 형, 오빠, 남동생

"You are not my _____,"
says Crocodile. (p.103)

call (전화를 걸어) 부르다

Dr. Roger _____s Fix Man. (p.30)

cheer 환호하다

"You fixed it!" Dr. Roger _____s.
(p.40)

come 오다

Fix Man _____s to school. (p.31)

cook 요리사

_____s work in the kitchen. (p.50)

cry 울다, 외치다

"Ouch!" Mina _____cries_____. (p.76)

d

doctor 의사

They help _____s. (p.15)

 egg 알

"A crocodile lays _____s," says Hen. (p.112)

f

fast 빠른

They move very _____. (p.88)

feather 털, 깃털

"You have _____s." (p.111)

finger 손가락

It twinkles on her _____. (p.58)

fix 수리하다

But he can not _____ it. (p.31)

flour 밀가루

Mia pours _____ into the bowl. (p.67)

h

happy 기쁜, 행복한

Everyone is _____. (p.22)

hard 단단한, 딱딱한

They have _____ skin. (p.87)

hospital 병원

We see robots in the _____.
(p.15)

house 집

We see robots in the _____.
(p.17)

hurry 서두르다

"Please _____!" (p.30)

j

jaw 턱

They have a strong _____. (p.86)

kitchen 부엌

Cooks work in the _____. (p.50)

land 육지, 땅

"You live on _____." (p.103)

love 대단히 좋아하다, 사랑하다

"We _____ pancakes!" they say. (p.75)

meal 식사

They make tasty _____s. (p.53)

meet 만나다

One day, Crocodile and Hen _____ at the river. (p.94)

milk 우유

Mia pours _____ into the bowl. (p.67)

122

mouth 입

Crocodile opens his _____. (p.95)

open 열다, 벌리다

Crocodile _____s his mouth.
(p.95)

point 가리키다

A kid _____s and asks, "What is this?" (p.38)

pour 붓다, 따르다

Mia _____s flour into the bowl. (p.67)

ring 반지

Mia likes her _____. (p.58)

robot 로봇

Where do you see _____s? (p.15)

run 달리다

"_____!" Dr. Roger says. (p.41)

sad 슬픈

Dr. Roger is _____. (p.38)

scale 비늘

"I have _____s," says Crocodile.
(p.110)

school 학교

Dr. Roger comes to _____. (p.22)

shut 닫다, 감다, 다물다

Crocodile _____s his mouth.
(p.97)

sister 언니, 누나, 여동생

Mia's _____, Mina, bites the
pancakes. (p.74)

sleep (잠을) 자다

She _____s with her ring on.
(p.60)

walk 걷다

"_____!" Dr. Roger says. (p.23)

water 물

"I live in _____," says Crocodile.
(p.102)

wear 끼고 있다, 입고 있다

She _____s her ring all the
time. (p.61)

webbed 물갈퀴가 있는

They have four _____ feet. (p.87)

wonder 궁금해하다

"Brother?" Crocodile _____s.
(p.105)

진짜진짜

초등
영어 읽기

하브루타 워크북

2

SISO study

진짜진짜 초등 영어 읽기 하브루타 워크북 **2**

Contents

하브루타 워크북 이렇게 학습하세요.

학습 안내 동영상을
확인하세요.

❶ 먼저 스토리북을 학습하고 와요.

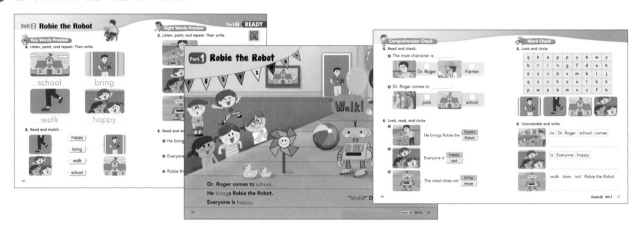

❷ 하브루타 워크북을 펴고 학습한 스토리북에 해당하는 하브루타 단어 와 하브루타 단어 연습 을 해요.

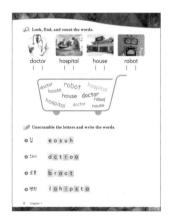

❸ 스토리 하나가 끝나면 하브루타 문장 에서 이야기에 대한 내용을 정리하고, 하브루타 3단계 질문 놀이 를 통해 북리포트는 작성합니다. LET'S THINK! 에서는 자유롭게 질문하고 답해요.

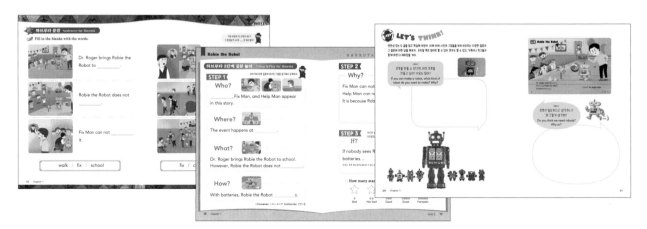

★ My Havruta Study Plan ★ 학습한 부분을 체크하고 날짜도 기록해 보세요.

	스토리북	워크북	학습한 날짜
Chapter 1 Unit **1** **Robots**	10~19p ☐	4~6p ☐	____ . ____
Chapter 1 Unit **2** Part 1 **Robie the Robot**	20~27p ☐	7~9p ☐	____ . ____
Chapter 1 Unit **2** Part 2 **Robie the Robot**	28~35p ☐	10~12p ☐	____ . ____
Chapter 1 Unit **2** Part 3 **Robie the Robot**	36~45p ☐	13~21p ☐	____ . ____
Chapter 2 Unit **1** **What a Cook Does**	46~55p ☐	22~24p ☐	____ . ____
Chapter 2 Unit **2** Part 1 **Pancakes and Mia's Ring**	56~63p ☐	25~27p ☐	____ . ____
Chapter 2 Unit **2** Part 2 **Pancakes and Mia's Ring**	64~71p ☐	28~30p ☐	____ . ____
Chapter 2 Unit **2** Part 3 **Pancakes and Mia's Ring**	72~81p ☐	31~39p ☐	____ . ____
Chapter 3 Unit **1** **Crocodiles**	82~91p ☐	40~42p ☐	____ . ____
Chapter 3 Unit **2** Part 1 **Crocodile and Hen**	92~99p ☐	43~45p ☐	____ . ____
Chapter 3 Unit **2** Part 2 **Crocodile and Hen**	100~107p ☐	46~48p ☐	____ . ____
Chapter 3 Unit **2** Part 3 **Crocodile and Hen**	108~117p ☐	49~57p ☐	____ . ____

Robots

 아래 단어를 큰 소리로 읽어 보자.
몇 번 읽고 싶니? 여기에 횟수를 적고,
큰 소리로 읽어 볼까?

• 읽을 횟수: _____

Look, check, and read aloud.

doctor 의사	 Easy Okay Difficult	**mom** 엄마	 Easy Okay Difficult

doctor
의사 Easy Okay Difficult

mom
엄마 Easy Okay Difficult

farm
농장

robot
로봇

help
돕다

see
보다

hospital
병원

where
어디에서

house
집

Write the words.

doctor
의사

hospital
병원

house
집

robot
로봇

외운 단어를 모두 적어보고, 힘들지 않게
잘 외워진 단어는 무엇인지 말해 볼까?

Look, find, and count the words.

doctor   hospital   house   robot

(   )   (   )   (   )   (   )

doctor   robot   hospital
house   house   doctor
hospital   doctor   robot
house

Unscramble the letters and write the words.

❶ 집   e o s u h

❷ 의사   d c t r o o

❸ 로봇   b r o o t

❹ 병원   l o h i p s t a

Robie the Robot

하브루타 단어 Words for Havruta

Look, check, and read aloud.

아래 단어를 큰 소리로 읽어 보자.
몇 번 읽고 싶니? 여기에 횟수를 적고,
큰 소리로 읽어 볼까?

• 읽을 횟수: _____

again 한 번 더, 다시	Easy	Okay	Difficult

happy 기쁜, 행복한	Easy Okay Difficult

bring
가져오다

move
움직이다

come
오다

say
말하다

Dr.
박사
(Doctor의 약어)

school
학교

everyone
모두

walk
걷다

Write the words.

bring

가져오다

happy

기쁜, 행복한

school

학교

walk

걷다

외우기 어려운 단어를 순서대로 3개만 써 봐.
왜 안 외워질까?

✏️ **Write the words correctly.**

bring

school

happy

walk

🔍 **Solve the puzzle.**

① → b [ ][ ][ ][ ]

④↓ w

③↓

② → s [ ] h [ ][ ]

① He b_____s Robie the Robot.

② Dr. Roger comes to s_____.

③ Everyone is h_____.

④ "W_____!" Dr. Roger says.

Robie the Robot

하브루타 단어 Words for Havruta

아래 단어를 큰 소리로 읽어 보자.
몇 번 읽고 싶니? 여기에 횟수를 적고,
큰 소리로 읽어 볼까?

• 읽을 횟수: _____

Look, check, and read aloud.

call
(전화를 걸어) 부르다

Easy Okay Difficult

hurry
서두르다

Easy Okay Difficult

can not
~할 수 없다

man
(성인) 남자

come
오다

please
부디, 제발

fix
수리하다

school
학교

help
돕다

Write the words.

call

(전화를 걸어) 부르다

come

오다

fix

수리하다

hurry

서두르다

'나만의 단어 외우는 방법'은 어떤 게 있을까?

 **Match the letters to the words.**

 · ·  ry · ·

 co · · ll · ·

 hur · · x · ·

ca · · me · ·

 **Cross out the wrong ones.**

 acll　　call　　call　　call

 fix　　fix　　fxi　　fix

 hurry　　hrury　　hurry　　hurry

 come　　come　　come　　cemo

하브루타 단어 Words for Havruta

아래 단어를 큰 소리로 읽어 보자.
몇 번 읽고 싶니? 여기에 횟수를 적고,
큰 소리로 읽어 볼까?

• 읽을 횟수: _____

Look, check, and read aloud.

ask
묻다

Easy Okay Difficult

point
가리키다

Easy Okay Difficult

everyone
모두

run
달리다

fix
수리하다

sad
슬픈

cheer
환호하다

walk
걷다

kid
아이

what
무엇

✏️ **Write the words.**

cheer

환호하다

point

가리키다

run

달리다

sad

슬픈

가장 좋아하는 단어를 쓰고,
빈 종이에 그림으로 그려보자.

Connect and write the words.

cheer •

point •

run •

sad •

• sad _____

• point _____

• run _____

• cheer _____

Cross out the wrong letters and write the words.

 p o i n t e _____

 s i a d _____

 c h i e e r _____

 r e u n _____

Fill in the blanks with the words.

Dr. Roger brings Robie the Robot to _____.

Robie the Robot does not _____.

Fix Man can not _____ it.

walk / fix / school

가장 마음에 드는 문장이 뭐니?
그 문장을 큰 소리로 _____번 읽어 볼까?

Help Man can not

_____ it.

Everyone is _____.

A kid fixes the robot.
Robie the Robot

_____s.
Everyone _____s.

fix / cheer / sad / run

Robie the Robot

STEP 1

이야기에 대한 질문에 주어진 그림을 참고해서 답해보자.

Who?

_____, Fix Man, and Help Man appear in this story.

Where?

The event happens at _____ .

What?

Dr. Roger brings Robie the Robot to school. However, Robie the Robot does not _____ .

How?

With batteries, Robie the Robot _____ s.

＊however 그러나, 하지만 batteries 건전지들

STEP 2

Why?

Fix Man can not fix the robot.

Help Man can not fix the robot.

It is because Robie the Robot has no _____.

STEP 3

If?

자신의 생각을 영어로 혹은
우리말로 자유롭게 이야기 해봐~

If nobody sees Robie the Robot has no

batteries...

아무도 로봇 로비에게 배터리가 없다는 걸 모른다면…

☐ **How many stars do you give this story?**

☆	☆☆	☆☆☆	☆☆☆☆	☆☆☆☆☆
Bad	Not bad	Good	Great	Fantastic

연관성 있는 두 글을 읽고 학습해 보았어. 이제 아래 사진과 그림들을 보며 떠오르는 다양한 질문과 그 질문에 대한 답을 해보자. 우리말 혹은 영어로 할 수 있어. 혼자도 할 수 있고, 가족이나 친구들과 함께 하면 더 재미있을 거야.

（예시）
로봇을 만들 수 있다면, 어떤 로봇을
만들고 싶어? 이유는 뭐야?

If you could make a robot, what kind of
robot would you want to make? Why?

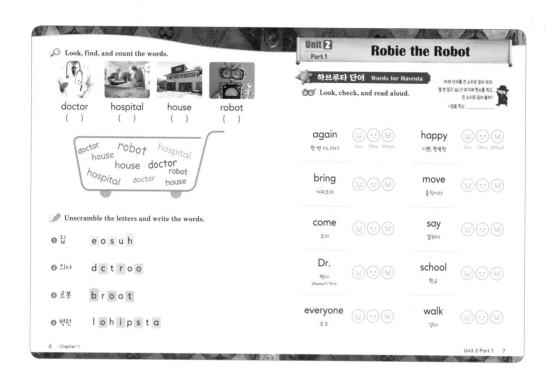

(예시)

로봇이 필요하다고 생각하니?
왜 그렇게 생각해?

Do you think we need robots?
Why?

What a Cook Does

하브루타 단어 **Words for Havruta**

 아래 단어를 큰 소리로 읽어 보자. 몇 번 읽고 싶니? 여기에 횟수를 적고, 큰 소리로 읽어 볼까?

• 읽을 횟수: _____

Look, check, and read aloud.

apron 앞치마	Easy Okay Difficult	keep 유지하다	Easy Okay Difficult
clean 깨끗한		kitchen 부엌	
cook 요리사		make 만들다	
food 음식		meal 식사	
fresh 신선한		prepare 준비하다, 마련하다	
hand 손		tasty 맛있는	
hat 모자		their 그들의	

wear
입다

 Easy Okay Difficult

work
일하다

 Easy Okay Difficult

하브루타 단어 연습 Word Practice for Havruta

 Write the words.

apron

앞치마

cook

요리사

kitchen

부엌

meal

식사

'나만의 단어 외우는 방법'은 어떤 게 있을까?

Look, find, and count the words.

apron	cook	kitchen	meal
( )	( )	( )	( )

cook apron meal cook
meal kitchen meal
apron cook apron apron
cook

Unscramble the letters and write the words.

❶ 식사   e l m a   _____

❷ 앞치마   n r p o a   _____

❸ 부엌   c e n h k t i   _____

❹ 요리사   o k o c   _____

Pancakes and Mia's Ring

하브루타 단어 Words for Havruta

아래 단어를 큰 소리로 읽어 보자.
몇 번 읽고 싶니? 여기에 횟수를 적고,
큰 소리로 읽어 볼까?

• 읽을 횟수: _____

Look, check, and read aloud.

all the time 줄곧, 내내	Easy Okay Difficult	ring 반지	Easy Okay Difficult
eat 먹다		sleep (잠을) 자다	
finger 손가락		twinkle 반짝거리다	
like 좋아하다		wear 끼고 있다, 입고 있다	
pancake 팬케이크		with …와 함께	
play 놀다			

하브루타 단어 연습 Word Practice for Havruta

✏️ **Write the words.**

finger
손가락

ring
반지

sleep
(잠을) 자다

wear
끼고 있다, 입고 있다

외운 단어를 모두 적어보고, 힘들지 않게
잘 외워진 단어는 무엇인지 말해 볼까?

✏️ **Write the words correctly.**

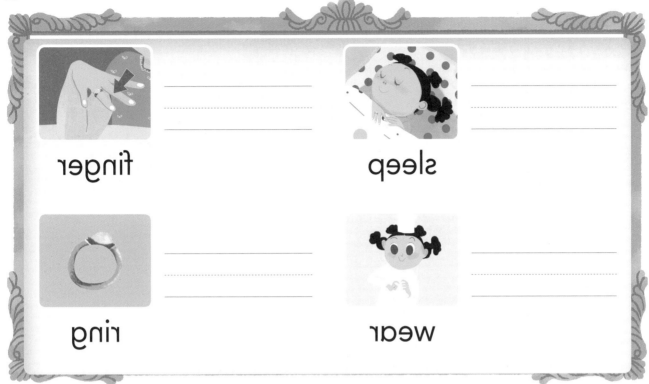

finger

sleep

ring

wear

🔍 **Solve the puzzle.**

❸↓ ❹↓

❶→ | w | | | r | | s |

❷→ | f | | | |

❶ She w_____s her ring all the time.

❷ It twinkles on her f_____.

❸ Mia likes her r_____.

❹ She s_____s with her ring on.

하브루타 단어 Words for Havruta

 Look, check, and read aloud.

 아래 단어를 큰 소리로 읽어 보자.
몇 번 읽고 싶니? 여기에 횟수를 적고,
큰 소리로 읽어 볼까?

• 읽을 횟수: _____

bowl 그릇	Easy Okay Difficult	**mix** 섞다
done 다 된, 완료된		**pancake** 팬케이크
flour 밀가루		**pour** 붓다, 따르다
make 만들다		**stir** 젓다, 섞다
milk 우유		**sugar** 설탕

Write the words.

bowl
그릇

flour
밀가루

milk
우유

pour
붓다, 따르다

외우기 어려운 단어를 순서대로 3개만 써 봐.
왜 안 외워질까?

 **Match the letters to the words.**

po

mi

fl

bo

ur

wl

lk

our

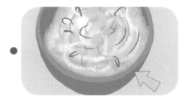

Cross out the wrong ones.

	pour	prou	pour	Pour
	mlik	milk	milk	milk
	bowl	bowl	bowl	bwol
	flour	flour	froul	flour

Pancakes and Mia's Ring

하브루타 단어 Words for Havruta

 Look, check, and read aloud.

아래 단어를 큰 소리로 읽어 보자.
몇 번 읽고 싶니? 여기에 횟수를 적고,
큰 소리로 읽어 볼까?

• 읽을 횟수: _____

bite		ouch	
베어 물다	Easy Okay Difficult	아야	Easy Okay Difficult
cook		ring	
요리사		반지	
cry		sister	
울다, 외치다		언니, 누나, 여동생	
dad		sorry	
아빠		미안한	
love		wear	
대단히 좋아하다, 사랑하다		끼고 있다, 입고 있다	

Write the words.

bite

베어 물다

cry

울다, 외치다

love

대단히 좋아하다, 사랑하다

sister

언니, 누나, 여동생

'나만의 단어 외우는 방법'은 어떤 게 있을까?

✏️ **Connect and write the words.**

sister •

cry •

love •

bite •

• love _____

• bite _____

• sister _____

• cry _____

✏️ **Cross out the wrong letters and write the words.**

 b a i t e _____

 s c i s t e r _____

 l o e v e _____

 c r a y _____

Fill in the blanks with the words.

Mia likes her _____ .

She _____s her ring all the time.

Mia and Mom make pancakes.
Mia _____s milk into the bowl.

wear / ring / pour

OO에게 들려주고 싶은 문장이 있니?
그 문장을 외워서 OO 앞에서
큰 소리로 말해 보자.

Now the _____s are done.

Mia's _____, Mina, bites the pancakes.

Mina cries.

It is Mia's ring.

Mom says, "A _____ does not wear a ring."

---

pancake / cook / sister

이야기에 대한 질문에 주어진 그림을 참고해서 답해보자.

STEP 1

Who?

_____, Mia's _____ and dad, and
Mia's _____, Mina, appear in this story.

Where?

The event happens in the _____.

What?

Mia makes _____s.
Mia's sister, Mina, bites it and cries.

How?

A cook does not wear a _____.
Mia feels sorry.

STEP 2

Why?

Mom says to Mia, "A cook does not wear a ring."

It is because Mia is a cook today, and Mia's ring was in the _____.

STEP 3

자신의 생각을 영어로 혹은 우리말로 자유롭게 이야기 해봐~

If?

If Mia is a cook in a restaurant...

미아가 식당의 요리사라면...

☐ **How many stars do you give this story?**

☆	☆☆	☆☆☆	☆☆☆☆	☆☆☆☆☆
Bad	Not bad	Good	Great	Fantastic

LET'S THINK!

연관성 있는 두 글을 읽고 학습해 보았어. 이제 아래 사진과 그림들을 보며 떠오르는 다양한 질문과 그 질문에 대한 답을 해보자. 우리말 혹은 영어로 할 수 있어. 혼자도 할 수 있고, 가족이나 친구들과 함께 하면 더 재미있을 거야.

(예시)
요리사에 대한 글을 읽었는데, 요리사는 어떤 일을 해?
You read stories about cooks. What do they do?

(예시)
요리사가 요리를 만들 때 뭐가 가장 중요할까?
What is the most important thing when a cook makes meals?

What a Cook Does

Cooks work in the kitchen.

They wear a hat.
They wear an apron.

hat

apron

Chapter 2 Unit 1   51

50

Part 1 Pancakes and Mia's Ring

Mia likes her ring.
It twinkles on her finger.
She eats with her ring on.

She plays with her ring on.

(예시)

요리가사 되고 싶니? 이유가 뭐야?

Do you want to be a cook?
Why or why not?

하브루타 단어   Words for Havruta

Look, check, and read aloud.

아래 단어를 큰 소리로 읽어 보자.
몇 번 읽고 싶니? 여기에 횟수를 적고,
큰 소리로 읽어 볼까?

• 읽을 횟수: _____

animal 동물	Easy Okay Difficult
big 큰	
crocodile 악어	
dangerous 위험한	
fast 빠른	
feet 발 (foot의 복수형)	
four 4, 넷	

hard 단단한, 딱딱한	Easy Okay Difficult
jaw 턱	
live 살다	
river 강	
sharp 날카로운	
skin 피부, 가죽	
strong 튼튼한, 강한	

teeth
이, 치아
(tooth의 복수형)

 Easy Okay Difficult

webbed
물갈퀴가 있는

 Easy Okay Difficult

 하브루타 단어 연습 Word Practice for Havruta

 Write the words.

fast
빠른

hard
단단한, 딱딱한

jaw
턱

webbed
물갈퀴가 있는

가장 좋아하는 단어를 쓰고,
빈 종이에 그림으로 그려보자.

Look, find, and count the words.

fast   hard   jaw   webbed

(   )   (   )   (   )   (   )

jaw   hard   jaw   fast
fast   fast   hard   hard
hard   webbed   jaw
fast

Unscramble the letters and write the words.

❶ 단단한, 딱딱한   r a h d   _____

❷ 턱   w j a   _____

❸ 물갈퀴가 있는   d b b e e w   _____

❹ 빠른   f s t a   _____

Crocodile and Hen

하브루타 단어 Words for Havruta

Look, check, and read aloud.

아래 단어를 큰 소리로 읽어 보자.
몇 번 읽고 싶니? 여기에 횟수를 적고,
큰 소리로 읽어 볼까?

• 읽을 횟수: _____

brother

형, 오빠, 남동생

Easy　Okay　Difficult

mouth

입

Easy　Okay　Difficult

crocodile

악어

open

열다, 벌리다

eat

먹다

river

강

hen

암탉

shut

닫다, 감다, 다물다

meet

만나다

wonder

궁금해하다

✏️ **Write the words.**

meet
만나다

mouth
입

open
열다, 벌리다

shut
닫다, 감다, 다물다

외운 단어를 모두 적어보고, 힘들지 않게
잘 외워진 단어는 무엇인지 말해 볼까?

✏️ **Write the words correctly.**

meet _____

open _____

mouth _____

shut _____

🔍 **Solve the puzzle.**

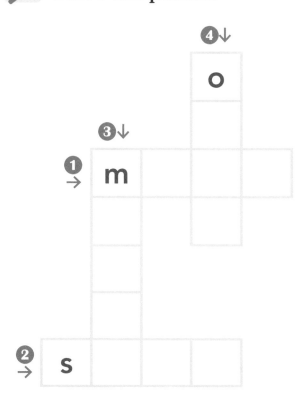

① One day, Crocodile and Hen m_____ at the river.

② Crocodile s_____s his mouth.

③ Crocodile opens his m_____.

④ Crocodile o_____s his mouth.

Crocodile and Hen

하브루타 단어   Words for Havruta

 Look, check, and read aloud.

아래 단어를 큰 소리로 읽어 보자.
몇 번 읽고 싶니? 여기에 횟수를 적고,
큰 소리로 읽어 볼까?

• 읽을 횟수: _____

	Easy	Okay	Difficult
brother 형, 오빠, 남동생	☺	😐	😫
crocodile 악어	☺	😐	😫
Don't~ ~하지 말아라	☺	😐	😫
hen 암탉	☺	😐	😫
land 육지, 땅	☺	😐	😫

	Easy	Okay	Difficult
live 살다	☺	😐	😫
say 말하다	☺	😐	😫
water 물	☺	😐	😫
will ~일(할) 것이다	☺	😐	😫
wonder 궁금해하다	☺	😐	😫

Write the words.

brother

형, 오빠, 남동생

land

육지, 땅

water

물

wonder

궁금해하다

외우기 어려운 단어를 순서대로 3개만 써 봐.
왜 안 외워질까?

Match the letters to the words.

 • •  • •

 • • ther • •

 • • nd • •

 • • der • •

 Cross out the wrong ones.

 water   awter   water   water

 land   land   land   danl

 brethor   brother   brother   brother

 wonder   wonder   onwder   wonder

Crocodile and Hen

하브루타 단어 Words for Havruta

Look, check, and read aloud.

아래 단어를 큰 소리로 읽어 보자.
몇 번 읽고 싶니? 여기에 횟수를 적고,
큰 소리로 읽어 볼까?

• 읽을 횟수: _____

alike

(아주) 비슷한

Easy   Okay   Difficult

feather

털, 깃털

Easy   Okay   Difficult

brother

형, 오빠, 남동생

goodbye

안녕 (작별 인사)

cry out

외치다

have

가지고 있다

eat

먹다

lay

알을 낳다

egg

알

scale

비늘

✎ **Write the words.**

alike

(아주) 비슷한

egg

알

feather

털, 깃털

scale

비늘

'나만의 단어 외우는 방법'은 어떤 게 있을까?

✏️ **Connect and write the words.**

scale •

• alike _____

feather •

• scale _____

alike •

• feather _____

egg •

• egg _____

✏️ **Cross out the wrong letters and write the words.**

f e a t h d e r _____

s c a i l e _____

a l a i k e _____

e g e g _____

Fill in the blanks with the words.

Crocodile and Hen meet at the river.

"I will eat you!" says

_____.

"Don't eat me, my

_____!" says Hen.

"I live in _____.
You live on _____.
You are not my brother,"
says Crocodile.

water / brother / Crocodile / land

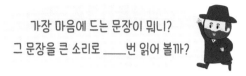

가장 마음에 드는 문장이 뭐니?
그 문장을 큰 소리로 ____번 읽어 볼까?

"Don't eat me, my brother!" says Hen.

"I have _____s. You have _____s," says Crocodile.

"A crocodile lays eggs. A hen lays eggs. We are _____!" says Hen.

feather / scale / alike

Crocodile and Hen

STEP 1

이야기에 대한 질문에 주어진 그림을 참고해서 답해보자.

Who?

_____ and _____ appear in this story.

Where?

The event happens at the _____.

What?

Crocodile wants to eat Hen.
Hen says Crocodile is her _____.

How?

Hen insists Crocodile and Hen are _____
because they both lay eggs.

* insist 주장하다

STEP 2

Why?

Crocodile thinks he is not Hen's brother.

It is because _____

_____ .

Hen thinks Crocodile is her brother.

It is because _____

_____ .

STEP 3

자신의 생각을 영어로 혹은
우리말로 자유롭게 이야기 해봐~

If?

If one of them does not lay eggs…

악어나 암탉 중 하나가 알을 낳지 않는다면…

☐ **How many stars do you give this story?**

☆	☆☆	☆☆☆	☆☆☆☆	☆☆☆☆☆
Bad	Not bad	Good	Great	Fantastic

연관성 있는 두 글을 읽고 학습해 보았어. 이제 아래 사진과 그림들을 보며 떠오르는 다양한 질문과 그 질문에 대한 답을 해보자. 우리말 혹은 영어로 할 수 있어. 혼자도 할 수 있고, 가족이나 친구들과 함께 하면 더 재미있을 거야.

(예시)
악어를 좋아하니? 이유가 뭐야?
Do you like crocodiles? Why or why not?

(예시)
악어에 대해 어떤 걸 알고 있니?
What do you know about crocodiles?

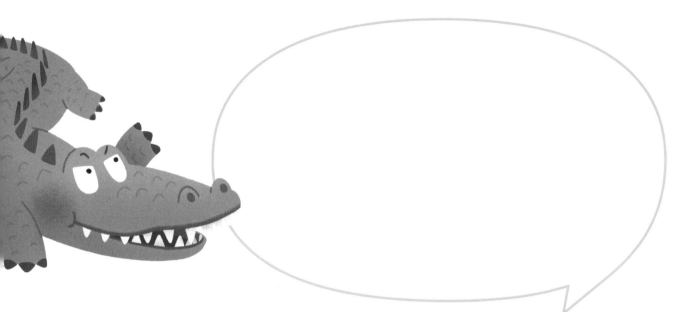

(예시)

악어와 암탉 이야기에 나오는 악어에 대해
어떻게 생각하니?

In the story "Crocodile and Hen",
what do you think of Crocodile?

Storybook 2 정답

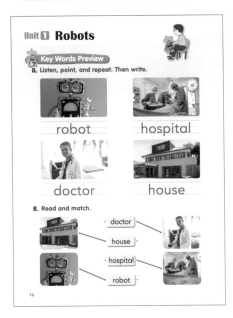

Unit 1 Robots

Key Words Preview

A. Listen, point, and repeat. Then write.

robot

hospital

doctor

house

B. Read and match.

· doctor

house ·

· hospital

robot ·

12

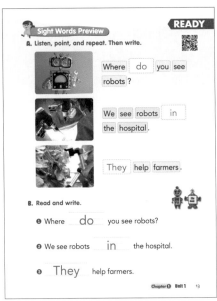

Sight Words Preview

A. Listen, point, and repeat. Then write.

Where | do | you | see | robots ?

We | see | robots | in | the | hospital .

They | help | farmers .

B. Read and write.

❶ Where __do__ you see robots?

❷ We see robots __in__ the hospital.

❸ __They__ help farmers.

Chapter ① Unit 1   13

Comprehension Check

A. Read and check.

❶ This is a story about _____.

✓ robots   farmers

❷ We see robots in the _____.

✓ hospital   woods

B. Look and check T(True) or F(False).

❶ We see robots on the farm.   T ✓ F

❷ We see robots in the house.   T ✓ F

❸ They help farmers.   T   F ✓

18

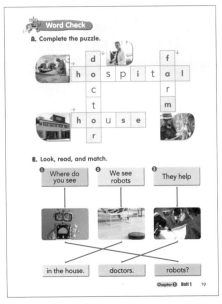

Word Check

A. Complete the puzzle.

```
        d           f
h o s p i t a l     
    c           r
    t           m
h o u s e
    r
```

B. Look, read, and match.

❶ Where do you see   ❷ We see robots   ❸ They help

in the house.   doctors.   robots?

Chapter ① Unit 1   19

Unit 2 Robie the Robot

Key Words Preview

A. Listen, point, and repeat. Then write.

school

bring

walk

happy

B. Read and match.

happy ·

bring ·

walk ·

school ·

20

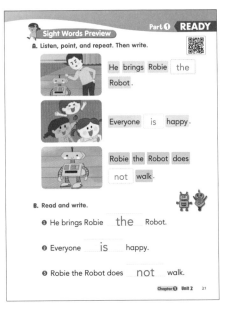

Part ① READY

Sight Words Preview

A. Listen, point, and repeat. Then write.

He | brings | Robie | the | Robot .

Everyone | is | happy .

Robie | the | Robot | does | not | walk .

B. Read and write.

❶ He brings Robie __the__ Robot.

❷ Everyone __is__ happy.

❸ Robie the Robot does __not__ walk.

Chapter ① Unit 2   21

Comprehension Check

A. Read and check.

❶ The main character is _____.

✓ Dr. Roger   Farmer

❷ Dr. Roger comes to _____.

park   ✓ school

B. Look, read, and circle.

❶ He brings Robie the   Doctor / **Robot**

❷ Everyone is   **happy** / sad

❸ The robot does not   bring / **move**

26

Word Check

A. Look and circle.

```
q  h  a  p  p  y  b  w  y
b  r  i  n  g  f  d  a  k
z  x  c  b  v  m  b  l  j
q  s  c  h  o  o  l  k  k
p  w  z  b  m  v  c  f  h
```

B. Unscramble and write.

to | Dr. Roger | school | comes
Dr. Roger comes to school

is | Everyone | happy
Everyone is happy

walk | does | not | Robie the Robot
Robie the Robot does not walk

Chapter ① Unit 2   27

Unit 2 Robie the Robot

Key Words Preview

A. Listen, point, and repeat. Then write.

hurry

call

come

fix

B. Read and match.

· hurry

come ·

· call

fix ·

28

58

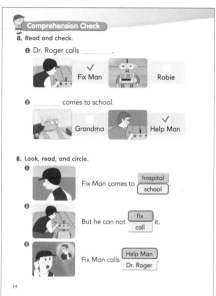

Panel 1 (page 29)

Sight Words Preview — Part 2 READY

A. Listen, point, and repeat. Then write.

Fix Man comes to school.

But he can not fix it.

But he can not fix it.

B. Read and write.

❶ Fix Man comes to school.

❷ But he can not fix it.

❸ But he can not fix it.

Chapter 1 Unit 2 29

Panel 2 (page 34)

Comprehension Check

A. Read and check.

❶ Dr. Roger calls _____.
✓ Fix Man   Robie

❷ _____ comes to school.
Grandma   ✓ Help Man

B. Look, read, and circle.

❶ Fix Man comes to [hospital / **school**]

❷ But he can not [**fix** / call] it.

❸ Fix Man calls [**Help Man** / Dr. Roger]

34

Panel 3 (page 35)

Word Check

A. Look and circle.

(hurry) w z q p k

t x c v (call) v x

f v c p m q (come)

w q z (fix) b v z p

B. Look, read, and match.

❶ Fix Man calls   ❷ Fix Man comes   ❸ Help Man can not

to school.   Help Man.   fix it.

Chapter 1 Unit 2 35

Panel 4 (page 36)

Unit 2 Robie the Robot

Key Words Preview

A. Listen, point, and repeat. Then write.

sad   point

cheer   run

B. Read and match.

point
run
cheer
sad

36

Panel 5 (page 37)

Sight Words Preview — Part 3 READY

A. Listen, point, and repeat. Then write.

Everyone is sad.

You fixed it.

Fix Man and Help Man cheer.

B. Read and write.

❶ Everyone is sad.

❷ You fixed it.

❸ Fix Man and Help Man cheer.

Chapter 1 Unit 2 37

Panel 6 (page 42)

Comprehension Check

A. Read and check.

❶ "You fixed it!" _____ cheers.
✓ Dr. Roger   Robie

❷ Fix Man and Help Man _____.
✓ cheer   call

B. Look, read, and check.

❶ ✓ A kid points and asks, "What is this?"
☐ A farmer points and asks, "What is this?"

❷ ☐ Robie the Robot says.
✓ Robie the Robot runs.

❸ ✓ Everyone cheers.
☐ Everyone is sad.

42

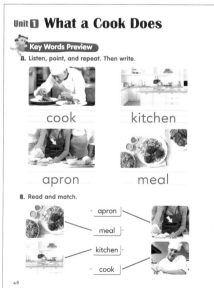

Panel 7 (page 43)

Word Check

A. Look and circle.

cheer (sad) run

sad cheer (point)

run point (cheer)

point (run) kid

B. Unscramble and write.

fixed You it
You fixed it

sad Everyone is
Everyone is sad

Robie runs Robot the
Robie the Robot runs

Chapter 1 Unit 2 43

Panel 8 (page 48)

Unit 1 What a Cook Does

Key Words Preview

A. Listen, point, and repeat. Then write.

cook   kitchen

apron   meal

B. Read and match.

apron
meal
kitchen
cook

48

Panel 9 (page 49)

Sight Words Preview — READY

A. Listen, point, and repeat. Then write.

Cooks work in the kitchen.

They wear a hat.

They make tasty meals.

B. Read and write.

❶ Cooks work in the kitchen.

❷ They wear a hat.

❸ They make tasty meals.

Chapter 2 Unit 1 49

Storybook 2 정답

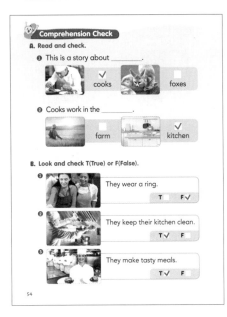

Comprehension Check

A. Read and check.
❶ This is a story about _____.
cooks ✓ foxes

❷ Cooks work in the _____.
farm kitchen ✓

B. Look and check T(True) or F(False).
❶ They wear a ring. T F ✓
❷ They keep their kitchen clean. T ✓ F
❸ They make tasty meals. T ✓ F

54

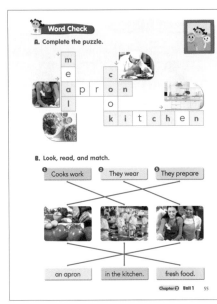

Word Check

A. Complete the puzzle.

```
  m
  e      c
a p r o n
  l      o
  k i t c h e n
```

B. Look, read, and match.
Cooks work / They wear / They prepare
an apron / in the kitchen. / fresh food.

Chapter 2 Unit 1 55

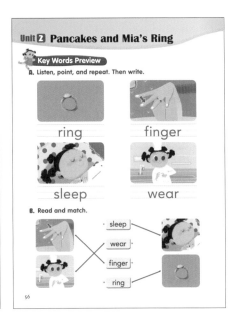

Unit 2 Pancakes and Mia's Ring

Key Words Preview

A. Listen, point, and repeat. Then write.

ring finger
sleep wear

B. Read and match.
sleep
wear
finger
ring

56

Sight Words Preview Part ❶ READY

A. Listen, point, and repeat. Then write.

It twinkles on her finger.

She eats with her ring on.

She plays with her ring on.

B. Read and write.
❶ It twinkles on her finger.
❷ She eats with her ring on.
❸ She plays with her ring on.

Chapter 2 Unit 2 57

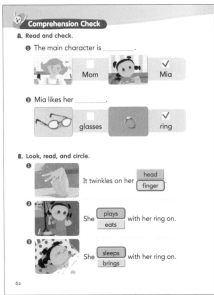

Comprehension Check

A. Read and check.
❶ The main character is _____.
Mom Mia ✓

❷ Mia likes her _____.
glasses ring ✓

B. Look, read, and circle.
❶ It twinkles on her head / finger
❷ She plays / eats with her ring on.
❸ She sleeps / brings with her ring on.

62

Word Check

A. Look and circle.

```
r i n g z x c u w
m b p y w v v t e
h f i n g e r m a
p q w z c b t k r
l j g s l e e p k
```

B. Unscramble and write.
Mia ring likes her
Mia likes her ring

with her ring on She plays
She plays with her ring on

She with eats her ring on
She eats with her ring on

Chapter 2 Unit 2 63

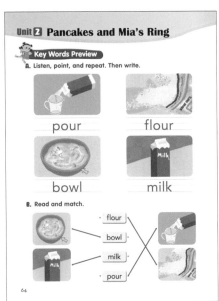

Unit 2 Pancakes and Mia's Ring

Key Words Preview

A. Listen, point, and repeat. Then write.

pour flour
bowl milk

B. Read and match.
flour
bowl
milk
pour

64

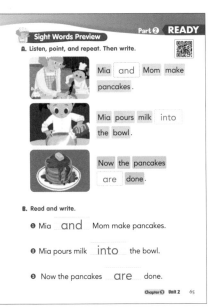

Sight Words Preview Part ❷ READY

A. Listen, point, and repeat. Then write.

Mia and Mom make pancakes.

Mia pours milk into the bowl.

Now the pancakes are done.

B. Read and write.
❶ Mia and Mom make pancakes.
❷ Mia pours milk into the bowl.
❸ Now the pancakes are done.

Chapter 2 Unit 2 65

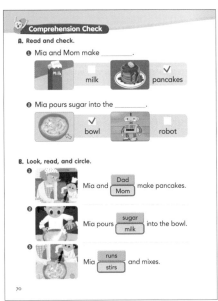

Comprehension Check

A. Read and check.
❶ Mia and Mom make _____.
milk pancakes ✓

❷ Mia pours sugar into the _____.
bowl ✓ robot

B. Look, read, and circle.
❶ Mia and Dad / Mom make pancakes.
❷ Mia pours sugar / milk into the bowl.
❸ Mia runs / stirs and mixes.

70

60

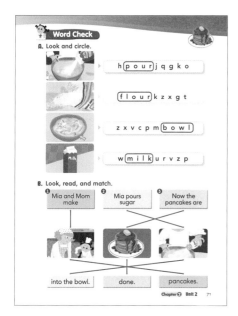

Word Check

A. Look and circle.

h p o u r j q g k o

f l o u r k z x g t

z x v c p m b o w l

w m i l k u r v z p

B. Look, read, and match.

1 Mia and Mom make
2 Mia pours sugar
3 Now the pancakes are

into the bowl. done. pancakes.

Chapter 2 Unit 2 71

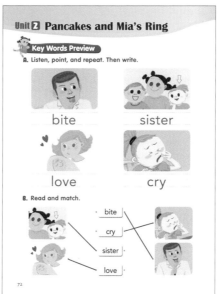

Unit 2 Pancakes and Mia's Ring

Key Words Preview

A. Listen, point, and repeat. Then write.

bite sister

love cry

B. Read and match.

· bite
· cry
sister
love ·

72

Sight Words Preview

A. Listen, point, and repeat. Then write.

Dad bites the pancakes .

We love pancakes !

That is my ring !

B. Read and write.

❶ Dad bites the pancakes.

❷ We love pancakes!

❸ That is my ring!

Chapter 2 Unit 2 73

Comprehension Check

A. Read and check.

❶ "Ouch!" _____ cries.

Dad ✓ Mina

❷ "That is my _____!" Mia says.

✓ ring pancakes

B. Look, read, and check.

❶ ✓ Dad bites the pancakes.
☐ Mom bites the pancakes.

❷ We love robots!
✓ We love pancakes!

❸ ✓ A cook does not wear a ring.
☐ A kid does not wear a ring.

78

Word Check

A. Look and circle.

sister (bite) cry   cry love (sister)

bite sister (love)   love bite (cry)

B. Unscramble and write.

the Dad pancakes bites

Dad bites the pancakes

is That ring my

That is my ring !

pancakes We love

We love pancakes !

Chapter 2 Unit 2 79

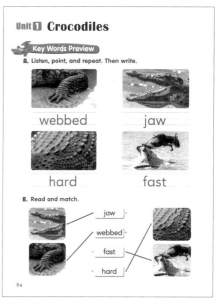

Unit 1 Crocodiles

Key Words Preview

A. Listen, point, and repeat. Then write.

webbed jaw

hard fast

B. Read and match.

jaw ·
webbed ·
· fast
· hard

84

Sight Words Preview

A. Listen, point, and repeat. Then write.

Crocodiles are big animals .

They have a strong jaw .

They live in rivers .

B. Read and write.

❶ Crocodiles are big animals.

❷ They have a strong jaw.

❸ They live in rivers.

Chapter 3 Unit 1 85

Comprehension Check

A. Read and check.

❶ This is a story about a _____.

✓ crocodile fox

❷ Crocodiles live in _____.

woods ✓ rivers

B. Look and check T(True) or F(False).

❶ They have a strong jaw.
T ✓ F

❷ They have hard feet.
T F ✓

❸ They hunt very fast.
T ✓ F

90

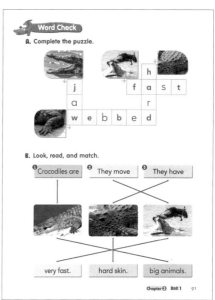

Word Check

A. Complete the puzzle.

h
j f a s t
a r
w e b b e d

B. Look, read, and match.

❶ Crocodiles are ❷ They move ❸ They have

very fast. hard skin. big animals.

Chapter 3 Unit 1 91

Storybook 정답 **61**

Storybook 2 정답

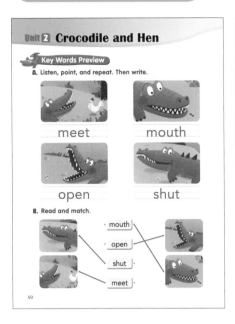

Unit 2 Crocodile and Hen

Key Words Preview

A. Listen, point, and repeat. Then write.

meet   mouth

open   shut

B. Read and match.

· mouth
· open
shut ·
meet ·

92

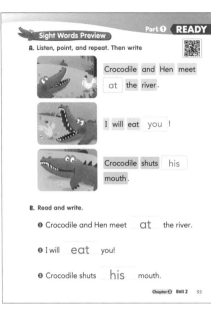

Sight Words Preview   Part 1 **READY**

A. Listen, point, and repeat. Then write.

Crocodile and Hen meet at the river.

I will eat you !

Crocodile shuts his mouth.

B. Read and write.

❶ Crocodile and Hen meet at the river.

❷ I will eat you!

❸ Crocodile shuts his mouth.

Chapter 3 Unit 2 93

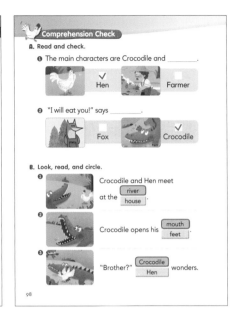

Comprehension Check

A. Read and check.

❶ The main characters are Crocodile and _____.

✓ Hen   Farmer

❷ "I will eat you!" says _____.

Fox   ✓ Crocodile

B. Look, read, and circle.

❶ Crocodile and Hen meet at the [river / house]

❷ Crocodile opens his [mouth / feet]

❸ "Brother?" [Crocodile / Hen] wonders.

98

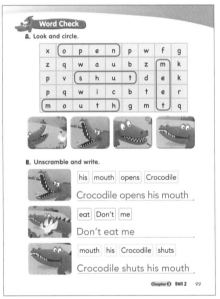

Word Check

A. Look and circle.

x	o	p	e	n	p	w	f	g
z	q	w	a	u	b	z	m	k
p	v	s	h	u	t	d	e	k
p	q	w	i	c	b	t	e	r
m	o	u	t	h	g	m	t	q

B. Unscramble and write.

his mouth opens Crocodile

Crocodile opens his mouth

eat Don't me

Don't eat me

mouth his Crocodile shuts

Crocodile shuts his mouth

Chapter 3 Unit 2 99

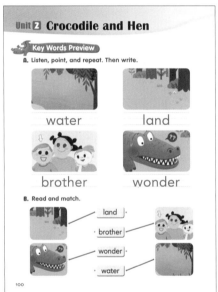

Unit 2 Crocodile and Hen

Key Words Preview

A. Listen, point, and repeat. Then write.

water   land

brother   wonder

B. Read and match.

land ·
· brother
wonder ·
· water

100

Sight Words Preview   Part 2 **READY**

A. Listen, point, and repeat. Then write.

I live in water.

You live on land.

You are not my brother.

B. Read and write.

❶ I live in water.

❷ You live on land.

❸ You are not my brother.

Chapter 3 Unit 2 101

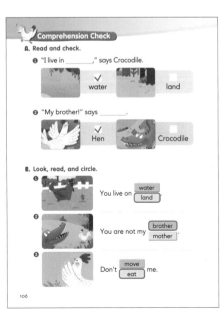

Comprehension Check

A. Read and check.

❶ "I live in _____," says Crocodile.

✓ water   land

❷ "My brother!" says _____.

✓ Hen   Crocodile

B. Look, read, and circle.

❶ You live on [water / land]

❷ You are not my [brother / mother]

❸ Don't [move / eat] me.

106

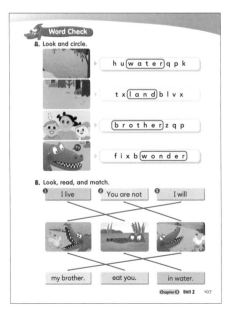

Word Check

A. Look and circle.

h u w a t e r q p k

t x l a n d b l v x

b r o t h e r z q p

f i x b w o n d e r

B. Look, read, and match.

❶ I live   ❷ You are not   ❸ I will

my brother.   eat you.   in water.

Chapter 3 Unit 2 107

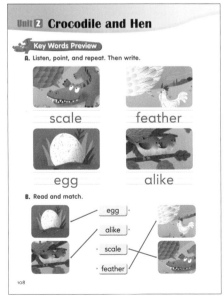

Unit 2 Crocodile and Hen

Key Words Preview

A. Listen, point, and repeat. Then write.

scale   feather

egg   alike

B. Read and match.

egg ·
alike ·
· scale
feather ·

108

62

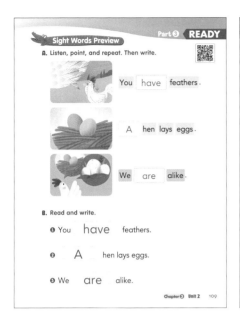

Sight Words Preview

A. Listen, point, and repeat. Then write.

You [have] feathers.

A [hen] lays eggs.

[We] [are] [alike].

B. Read and write.

❶ You **have** feathers.

❷ **A** hen lays eggs.

❸ We **are** alike.

Chapter ❸ **Unit 2**   109

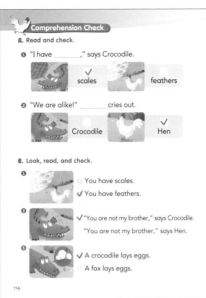

Comprehension Check

A. Read and check.

❶ "I have _____," says Crocodile.

✓ scales   feathers

❷ "We are alike!" _____ cries out.

Crocodile   ✓ Hen

B. Look, read, and check.

❶ ☐ You have scales.
   ✓ You have feathers.

❷ ✓ "You are not my brother," says Crocodile.
   ☐ "You are not my brother," says Hen.

❸ ✓ A crocodile lays eggs.
   ☐ A fox lays eggs.

114

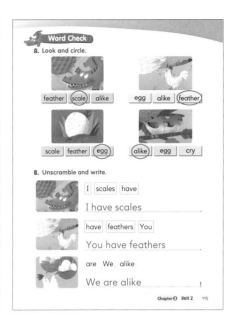

Word Check

A. Look and circle.

feather (scale) alike   egg alike (feather)

scale feather (egg)   (alike) egg cry

B. Unscramble and write.

[I] [scales] [have]
I have scales .

[have] [feathers] [You]
You have feathers .

[are] [We] [alike]
We are alike !

Chapter ❸ **Unit 2**   115

Storybook 정답   63

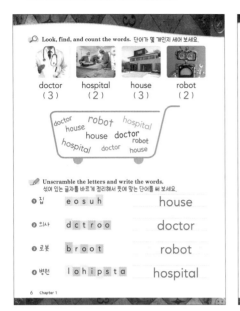

Look, find, and count the words. 단어가 몇 개인지 세어 보세요.

doctor (3)　hospital (2)　house (3)　robot (2)

doctor robot hospital
house house doctor robot
hospital doctor house

Unscramble the letters and write the words.
섞여 있는 글자를 바르게 정리해서 뜻에 맞는 단어를 써 보세요.

❶ 집　e o s u h　house

❷ 의사　d c t r o o　doctor

❸ 로봇　b r o o t　robot

❹ 병원　l o h i p s t a　hospital

6　Chapter 1

Write the words correctly. 단어를 바르게 써 보세요.

bring　school
happy　walk

Solve the puzzle. 퍼즐을 풀어 보세요.

❶ b r i n g
❷ s c h o o l
w a l k
h a p p y

❶ He b ring s Robie the Robot.
❷ Dr. Roger comes to chool.
❸ Everyone is h appy .
❹ "W alk !" Dr. Roger says.

Unit 2 Part 1　9

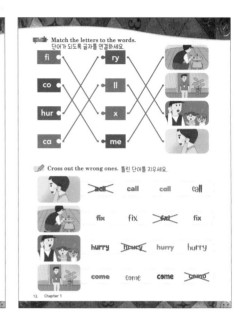

Match the letters to the words.
단어가 되도록 글자를 연결하세요.

fi　ry
co　ll
hur　x
ca　me

Cross out the wrong ones. 틀린 단어를 지우세요.

acll　call　call　call
fix　fix　fxit　fix
hurry　hrucy　hurry　hurry
come　come　come　comd

12　Chapter 1

Connect and write the words. 단어와 그림을 연결하고 써 보세요.

cheer　sad　sad
point　point　point
run　run　run
sad　cheer　cheer

Cross out the wrong letters and write the words.
잘못 들어간 글자를 지우고 올바른 단어를 써 보세요.

point e　point
s x a d　sad
ch x eer　cheer
r x u n　run

Unit 2 Part 3　15

하브루타 문장　Sentences for Havruta

Fill in the blanks with the words. 단어를 이용해 빈칸을 채워 보세요.

Dr. Roger brings Robie the Robot to school .
로저 박사님이 학교에 로봇 로비를 가져 와요.

Robie the Robot does not walk .
로봇 로비가 걷지 않아요.

Fix Man can not fix it.
픽스맨은 로봇 로비를 고치지 못해요.

walk / fix / school

16　Chapter 1

Help Man can not fix it.
헬프맨도 로봇 로비를 고치지 못해요.

Everyone is sad .
모두들 아쉬워해요.

A kid fixes the robot.
Robie the Robot run s.
Everyone cheer s.
한 아이가 그 로봇을 고쳐요.
로봇 로비가 뛰어요. 모두가 환호성을 질러요.

fix / cheer / sad / run

Unit 2　17

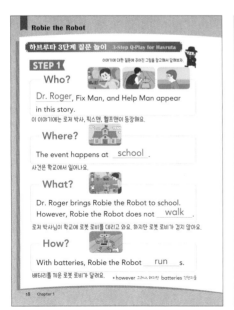

Robie the Robot

하브루타 3단계 질문 놀이　3-Step Q-Play for Havruta

STEP 1

Who?
Dr. Roger , Fix Man, and Help Man appear in this story.
이 이야기에는 로저 박사, 픽스맨, 헬프맨이 등장해요.

Where?
The event happens at school .
사건은 학교에서 일어나요.

What?
Dr. Roger brings Robie the Robot to school.
However, Robie the Robot does not walk .
로저 박사님이 학교에 로봇 로비를 데리고 와요. 하지만 로봇 로비가 걷지 않아요.

How?
With batteries, Robie the Robot run s.
배터리를 끼운 로봇 로비가 달려요.　*however 그러나, 하지만　batteries 건전지들

18　Chapter 1

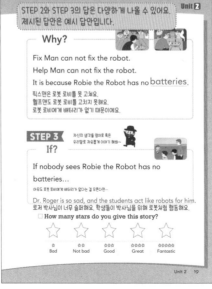

STEP 2와 STEP 3의 답은 다양하게 나올 수 있어요.
제시된 답안은 예시 답안입니다.

Why?
Fix Man can not fix the robot.
Help Man can not fix the robot.
It is because Robie the Robot has no batteries .
픽스맨도 로봇 로비를 못 고쳐요.
헬프맨도 로봇 로비를 고치지 못해요.
로봇 로비에게 배터리가 없기 때문이에요.

STEP 3
If?
자신의 생각을 열어 혹은 우리말로 자유롭게 이야기 해봐요~

If nobody sees Robie the Robot has no batteries...
아무도 로봇 로비에게 배터리가 없다는 걸 모른다면~
Dr. Roger is so sad, and the students act like robots for him.
로저 박사님이 너무 슬퍼해요. 학생들이 박사님을 위해 로봇처럼 행동해요.
☐ How many stars do you give this story?

☆ ☆ ☆ ☆ ☆
Bad　Not bad　Good　Great　Fantastic

Unit 2　19

Look, find, and count the words. 단어가 몇 개인지 세어 보세요.

apron (4)　cook (4)　kitchen (1)　meal (2)

cook apron meal cook
meal kitchen apron
apron cook apron cook

Unscramble the letters and write the words.
섞여 있는 글자를 바르게 정리해서 뜻에 맞는 단어를 써 보세요.

❶ 식사　e l m a　meal

❷ 앞치마　n r p o a　apron

❸ 부엌　c e n h k t i　kitchen

❹ 요리사　o k o c　cook

24　Chapter 2

Write the words correctly. 단어를 바르게 써 보세요.

finger
sleep
ring
wear

Solve the puzzle. 퍼즐을 풀어 보세요.

w e a r i n g
s l e e p
f i n g e r

❶ She w __ears__ s her ring all the time.
❷ It twinkles on her f __inger__ .
❸ Mia likes her __ring__ .
❹ She s __leep__ s with her ring on.

Unit 2 Part 1   27

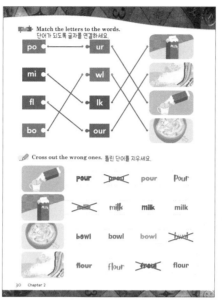

Match the letters to the words. 단어가 되도록 글자를 연결하세요.

po — ur
mi — wl
fl — lk
bo — our

Cross out the wrong ones. 틀린 단어를 지우세요.

pour ~~poer~~ pour pour
~~milk~~ milk milk milk
bowl bowl bowl ~~bowl~~
flour flour ~~flour~~ flour

30   Chapter 2

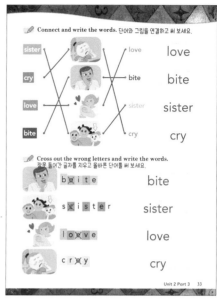

Connect and write the words. 단어와 그림을 연결하고 써 보세요.

sister — love
cry — bite
love — sister
bite — cry

love
bite
sister
cry

Cross out the wrong letters and write the words.
잘못 들어간 글자를 지우고 올바른 단어를 써 보세요.

b~~x~~ite → bite
s~~x~~ister → sister
lo~~x~~ve → love
cr~~x~~y → cry

Unit 2 Part 3   33

하브루타 문장 Sentences for Havruta

Fill in the blanks with the words. 단어를 이용해 빈칸을 채워 보세요.

Mia likes her __ring__ .
미아는 자신의 반지를 좋아해요.

She __wear__ s her ring all the time.
미아는 항상 반지를 끼고 있어요.

Mia and Mom make pancakes.
Mia __pour__ s milk into the bowl.
미아와 엄마가 팬케이크를 만들어요.
미아가 그릇에 우유를 부어요.

wear / ring / pour

34   Chapter 2

○○○에 들어가고 싶은 문장이 있나요?
그 문장을 의미와 ○○ 맞에서
큰 소리로 말해 보자.

Now the __pancake__ s are done.
이제 팬케이크가 완성되었어요.

Mia's __sister__ , Mina, bites the pancakes.
미아의 여동생 미나가 팬케이크를 한 입 베어 물어요.

Mina cries.
It is Mia's ring.
Mom says, "A __cook__ does not wear a ring."
미나가 울며 소리쳐요. 미아의 반지예요.
"요리사는 반지를 끼지 않아요!"라고 엄마가 말해요.

pancake / cook / sister

Unit 2   35

Pancakes and Mia's Ring

하브루타 3단계 질문 놀이 3-Step Q-Play for Havruta

STEP 1
이야기에 대한 질문에 주어진 그림을 참고하여 답해보자

Who?
__Mia__ , Mia's __mom__ and dad, and Mia's __sister__ , Mina, appear in this story.
이 이야기에는 미아, 미아의 엄마와 아빠, 그리고 미아의 여동생 미나가 나와요.

Where?
The event happens in the __kitchen__ .
사건은 부엌에서 일어나요.

What?
Mia makes __pancake__ s.
Mia's sister, Mina, bites it and cries.
미아가 팬케이크를 만들어요. 미아의 여동생, 미나가 한입 베어 물고 울어요.

How?
A cook does not wear a __ring__ .
Mia feels sorry.
요리사는 반지를 끼지 않아요. 미아는 미안해해요.

36   Chapter 2

STEP 2와 STEP 3의 답은 다양하게 나올 수 있어요.
제시된 답안은 예시 답안입니다.

Why?
Mom says to Mia, "A cook does not wear a ring."
It is because Mia is a cook today, and Mia's ring was in the __pancake__ .
엄마가 미아에게 말해요. "요리사는 반지를 끼지 않는단다."
미아가 오늘의 요리사인데, 미아의 반지가 팬케이크에서 나왔기 때문이에요.

STEP 3   자신의 생각을 말이로 혹은 요리말로 자유롭게 이야기 해보자~
If?
If Mia is a cook in a restaurant...
미아가 식당의 요리사라면...
Mia always wears gloves when she cooks.
미아는 요리할 때 항상 장갑을 낄 거예요.

☐ How many stars do you give this story?
☆ ☆ ☆ ☆ ☆
☆ Bad ☆☆ Not bad ☆☆☆ Good ☆☆☆☆ Great ☆☆☆☆☆ Fantastic

Unit 2   37

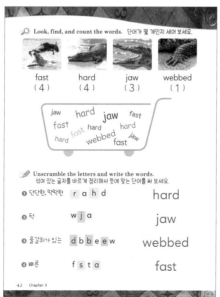

Look, find, and count the words. 단어가 몇 개인지 세어 보세요.

fast (4)   hard (4)   jaw (3)   webbed (1)

jaw hard jaw fast
fast fast hard hard
hard fast webbed jaw
webbed fast

Unscramble the letters and write the words.
섞여 있는 글자를 바르게 정리해서 뜻에 맞는 단어 써 보세요.

❶ 단단한, 딱딱한   r a h d   → hard
❷ 턱   w j a   → jaw
❸ 물갈퀴가 있는   d b b e e w   → webbed
❹ 빠른   f s t a   → fast

4.2   Chapter 3

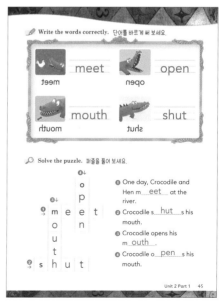

Write the words correctly. 단어를 바르게 써 보세요.

meet   open
mouth   shut

Solve the puzzle. 퍼즐을 풀어 보세요.

o p e n
m e e t
m o u t h
s h u t

❶ One day, Crocodile and Hen m __eet__ at the river.
❷ Crocodile s __hut__ s his mouth.
❸ Crocodile opens his m __outh__ .
❹ Crocodile o __pen__ s his mouth.

Unit 2 Part 1   45

Workbook 정답   65

Workbook 정답

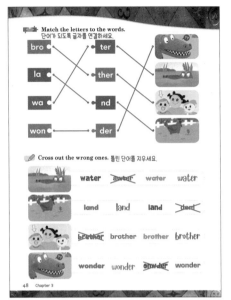

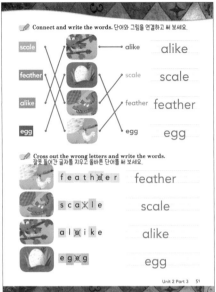

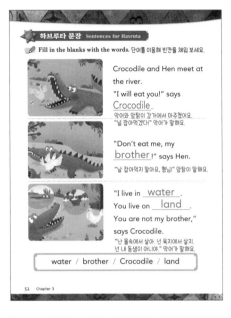

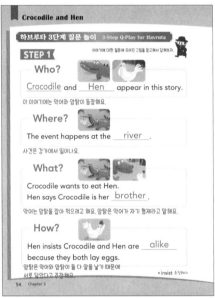

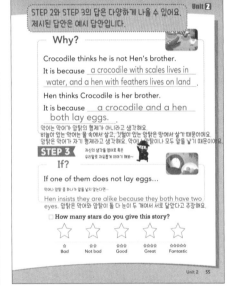

본문 해석

Chapter 1 Robots
Unit 1 Robots

Where do you see robots?
We see robots in the hospital.
They help doctors.
We see robots on the farm.
They help farmers.
We see robots in the house.
They help mom! (33)

로봇

어디에서 로봇을 볼 수 있을까요?
병원에서 로봇을 볼 수 있어요.
병원에서 로봇은 의사를 도와요.
농장에서 로봇을 볼 수 있어요.
농장에서 로봇은 농부를 도와요.
우리 집에서 로봇을 볼 수 있어요.
집에서 로봇은 엄마를 도와요!

Unit 2 Robie the Robot

Dr. Roger comes to school.
He brings Robie the Robot.
Everyone is happy.
"Walk!" Dr. Roger says.
Robie the Robot does not walk.
"Walk!" Dr. Roger says again.
But the robot does not move.
"Please hurry!"
Dr. Roger calls Fix Man.
Fix Man comes to school.
But he can not fix it.
"Please hurry!"
Fix Man calls Help Man.
Help Man comes to school.
But he can not fix it.
Dr. Roger is sad.
Everyone is sad.
A kid points and asks, "What is this?"
"You fixed it!" Dr. Roger cheers.
"You fixed it!" Fix Man and Help Man cheer.
"Run!" Dr. Roger says.
Robie the Robot runs.
Everyone cheers. (113)

로봇 로비

로저 박사님이 학교에 와요.
박사님이 로봇 로비를 데리고 와요.
모두 신났어요.
"걸어!"라고 박사님이 말해요.
로봇 로비가 걷지 않아요.
"걸어!"라고 박사님이 다시 말해요.
하지만 로봇 로비는 움직이지 않아요.
"서둘러 주세요!"
로저 박사님이 픽스맨(수리공)에게 전화를 해요.
픽스맨이 학교에 와요.
하지만 로봇 로비를 못 고쳐요.
"서둘러 주세요!"
픽스맨이 헬프맨(조수)을 불러요.
헬프맨이 학교에 와요.
하지만 로봇 로비를 고치지 못해요.
로저 박사님이 안타까워해요.
모두들 아쉬워해요.
한 아이가 무언가를 가리키며 물어요, "이게 뭐예요?"
"네가 고쳤어!" 로저 박사님이 신나서 소리쳐요.
"네가 고쳤구나!" 픽스맨와 헬프맨도 신나서 소리쳐요.
"뛰어!"라고 박사님이 말해요.
로봇 로비가 뛰어요.
모두가 환호성을 질러요.

Chapter 2 Cooking
Unit 1 What a Cook Does

Cooks work in the kitchen.
They wear a hat.
They wear an apron.
They keep their hands clean.
They keep their kitchen clean.
They prepare fresh food.
They make tasty meals. (35)

요리

요리사가 하는 일

요리사는 주방에서 일해요.
모자를 써요.
앞치마를 입어요.
손이 항상 깨끗해요.
주방을 청결하게 유지해요.
신선한 재료를 준비해요.
맛있는 식사를 요리해요.

Unit 2 Pancakes and Mia's Ring

Mia likes her ring.
It twinkles on her finger.
She eats with her ring on.
She plays with her ring on.
She sleeps with her ring on.
She wears her ring all the time.
Mia and Mom make pancakes.
Mia pours flour into the bowl.
Mia pours milk into the bowl.
Mia pours sugar into the bowl.
Mia stirs and mixes.
Now the pancakes are done.
Dad bites the pancakes.
Mia's sister, Mina, bites the pancakes, too.
"We love pancakes!" they say.
"Ouch!" Mina cries.
"That is my ring!" Mia says.
"A cook does not wear a ring," Mom says.
"I'm sorry," Mia says. (108)

팬케이크과 미아의 반지

미아는 자신의 반지를 정말 좋아해요.
반지가 미아의 손가락에서 반짝여요.
미아는 반지를 낀 채로 밥을 먹고
반지를 낀 채로 놀고
반지를 낀 채로 잠을 자요.
미아는 항상 반지를 끼고 있어요.
미아와 엄마가 팬케이크를 만들어요.
미아가 큰 그릇에 밀가루를 붓고
우유를 붓고
설탕을 부어요.
미아가 골고루 섞어요.
이제 팬케이크가 완성되었어요.
아빠가 팬케이크를 베어 먹어요.
미아 동생, 미나도 팬케이크를 베어 먹어요.
"팬케이크 너무 좋아!"라고 아빠와 미나가 말해요.
"아야!" 미나가 외쳐요.
"저건 내 반지잖아!" 미아가 말해요.
"요리사는 반지를 끼지 않아요!"라고 엄마가 말해요.
"죄송해요." 미아가 말해요.

Chapter 3 Crocodiles
Unit 1 Crocodiles

Crocodiles are big animals.
They have a strong jaw.
They have four webbed feet.
They have sharp teeth. They have hard skin.
They live in rivers.
They move very fast. They hunt very fast.
They can be very dangerous. (40)

악어

악어는 덩치가 큰 동물이에요.
악어는 턱이 튼튼하고
물갈퀴가 있는 발이 네 개에
날카로운 이빨과 딱딱한 피부를 가지고 있어요.
악어는 강에 살아요.
매우 빠르게 움직이고 재빠르게 사냥을 해요.
악어는 매우 위험할 수 있어요.

Unit 2 Crocodile and Hen

One day, Crocodile and Hen meet at the river.
"I will eat you!" says Crocodile.
Crocodile opens his mouth.
"My brother!" says Hen. "Don't eat me."
Crocodile shuts his mouth.
"Brother?" Crocodile wonders.
"I live in water" says Crocodile.
"You live on land."
"You are not my brother," says Crocodile.
"I will eat you!"
"My brother!" says Hen. "Don't eat me."
"Brother?" Crocodile wonders.
"I have scales," says Crocodile.
"You have feathers."
"You are not my brother," says Crocodile.
"I will eat you!"
"A crocodile lays eggs," says Hen, "and a hen lays eggs."
"We are alike!" Hen cries out. "Goodbye Brother!" (105)

악어와 암탉

어느 날 악어와 암탉이 강가에서 마주쳤어요.
"널 잡아먹겠다!" 악어가 말해요.
악어가 입을 쩍 벌려요.
"형님아!" 암탉이 말해요. "날 잡아먹지 말아요."
악어가 입을 다물어요.
"형님이라고?" 악어가 궁금해해요.
"나는 물 속에서 살아." 악어가 말해요.
"넌 땅에서 살지."
"넌 내 동생이 아니야." 악어가 말해요.
"널 잡아먹겠다!"
"형님아!" 암탉이 말해요. "날 잡아먹지 말아요."
"형님이라고?" 악어가 궁금해해요.
"난 비늘이 있어." 악어가 말해요.
"넌 깃털이 있지."
"넌 내 동생이 아니야." 악어가 말해요.
"널 잡아먹겠다!
"악어는 알을 낳아요." 암탉이 말해요. "암탉도 알을 낳죠."
"우린 닮았어요." 암탉이 소리쳐요. "잘 가요, 형님!"

초등
영어 읽기

하브루타 워크북
2